IVP *Crescendo*
COURAGE. CONFIDENCE. CALLING.

Some voices challenge us. Others support or encourage us. Voices can move us to change our minds, draw close to God, discover a new spiritual gift. The voices of others are shaping who we are.

The voices behind IVP Crescendo join together to draw us into God's story. We'll discover God's work around the globe even as we learn to love the people around the corner. We'll have opportunity to heal our places of pain. We'll discover new ways to love our families. We'll hear God's voice speaking into our lives as we discover new places of influence.

IVP Crescendo invites you to join in the rising chorus

- *to listen to the voices of others*
- *to hear the voice of God*
- *and to grow your own voice in*

COURAGE. CONFIDENCE. CALLING.

ivpress.com/crescendo
ivpress.com/crescendo-social

teach us to want

longing, ambition
& the life of faith

jen pollock michel

foreword by katelyn beaty

IVP Books

An imprint of InterVarsity Press
Downers Grove, Illinois

InterVarsity Press
P.O. Box 1400, Downers Grove, IL 60515-1426
www.ivpress.com
email@ivpress.com

InterVarsity Press® is the book-publishing division of InterVarsity Christian Fellowship/USA®, a movement of students and faculty active on campus at hundreds of universities, colleges and schools of nursing in the United States of America, and a member movement of the International Fellowship of Evangelical Students. For information about local and regional activities, write Public Relations Dept., InterVarsity Christian Fellowship/USA, 6400 Schroeder Rd., P.O. Box 7895, Madison, WI 53707-7895, or visit the IVCF website at www.intervarsity.org.

Scripture quotations, unless otherwise noted, are from The Holy Bible, English Standard Version, copyright © 2001 by Crossway Bibles, a division of Good News Publishers. Used by permission. All rights reserved.

While all stories in this book are true, some names and identifying information in this book have been changed to protect the privacy of the individuals involved.

Cover design: Cindy Kiple
Interior design: Beth Hagenberg
Images: Nancy Tamayo/Getty Images

ISBN 978-0-8308-4312-1 (print)
ISBN 978-0-8308-9633-2 (digital)

Printed in the United States of America ∞

Library of Congress Cataloging-in-Publication Data

Michel, Jen Pollock, 1974-
 Teach us to want : longing, ambition & the life of faith / Jen Pollock Michel.
  pages cm
 Includes bibliographical references.
 ISBN 978-0-8308-4312-1 (pbk. : alk. paper)
 1. Emotions—Religious aspects--Christianity. 2. Desire—Religious aspects--Christianity. 3. Desire for God. I. Title.
 BV4597.3.M53 2014
 233'.5—dc23

                                                                    2014013483

P	18	17	16	15	14	13	12	11	10	9	8	7	6	5		
Y	29	28	27	26	25	24	23	22	21	20	19	18	17	16	15

To my father,

Michael Kent Pollock (1944-1993)

"I haven't taken time lately to sit down

and write," your letter begins.

I have, Dad. Thanks to you.

Contents

There are two tragedies in life.
One is to lose your heart's desire.
The other is to gain it.

George Bernard Shaw, *Man and Superman*

❦

Thanks be to God, who in Christ always leads us
in triumphal procession, and through us spreads
the fragrance of the knowledge of him
everywhere. . . .Who is sufficient
for these things?

2 Corinthians 2:14, 16

Foreword

Of all the topics a Christian writer could take up in a land of plenty, you might think the last thing her audience would need is a book touting *desire*. Today's blaring headlines—on prime ministers' sex scandals, Wall Street Ponzi schemes, or the more mundane effects of materialism and gluttony—suggest that what our society needs most is self-control, not license to listen to our yearnings. As soon as sin-bent humans utter "I want," it seems, we open a door through which floods only personal and societal harm.

But what if "I want" trips off our tongues as easily as breath? What if, despite all the ways desire has been perverted and corroded down through human history, God actually made us for it?

Desire has been enjoying somewhat of a renaissance in theological circles. With his 2009 book, *Desiring the Kingdom: Worship, Worldview, and Cultural Formation*, philosopher James K. A. Smith challenged a Christian culture that casts discipleship as a dreary matter of thinking right thoughts and acting accordingly. On the contrary, says Smith, humans are "desiring agents," guided in life not by what we believe but by what we love. The business of following Christ, then, is about reorienting our loves and desires toward his kingdom. We need not just be convinced of Christ. We need to be *captivated by* him.

All well and good, and certainly in line with the most foundational theologian of Western thought, Augustine of Hippo. His *Confessions* opens with a statement of resonant, holy desire: "You have made us for yourself, O Lord, and our hearts are restless until they rest in you." C. S. Lewis went as far as to say (in his essay "The Weight of Glory") that if anything, our desires are not too strong but too *weak*, and that what God really wants to give us is infinite joy, a "holiday at the sea," his very self.

Really? God *wants* to give us joy? God *desires* to satisfy the deepest, most elemental aspects of our thirsty souls? When the sins and sufferings of our lives keep us aching and let down, how do we muster the courage to believe this?

With the book before you, Jen Pollock Michel has offered a practical theology of desire, a richly narrative exploration of longing. She bravely traces the moments of her life, and the lives of other women, in which "I want" seems a dangerous thing to utter before God. And she plants readers in the rich tradition of the Lord's Prayer, which allows us to both name our desires and let them be reoriented by the love and holiness of Christ.

It is appropriate, in only a providential way, that I am writing the introduction to Jen's book. The first time Jen and I met in person was in the summer of 2012, when Jen was visiting family in the Chicago suburbs. Jen had been writing for a website that I was editing, and at the time, desire was fresh on my heart and mind. In a couple hours over breakfast, I had detailed how a recent personal dream had fallen through the cracks and left me bereft. I had wrongly assumed that a beautiful and accomplished writer raising five children who speak French would not know of such things. As it turns out, to live on this earth means to know about desire dashed.

If you are reading this book, chances are you know about it too. Perhaps you desire something you have been afraid to name because it might set you up for more disappointment. Perhaps you can't name your desire because it seems selfish. (Christian women, in particular, may fall prey to the belief that asking, "What do I want?" is to neglect the holy responsibilities of family and ministry.) Perhaps you never thought that God intended his followers to desire, or that he desires *you*.

Amid these fears and hesitations, dear reader, I hope that with *Teach Us to Want*, Jen has modeled for you a boldness to name and voice your desires. To let God mold and recast them in the fires of his love and good purposes for you. To know that many others walk in the valley between what is longed for and what is realized. To say, with Christ, "thy will be done" with trust, confidence and, ultimately, joy.

Katelyn Beaty
Managing Editor, Christianity Today

1

Afraid to Want

Fear

It was the voice of God I was hearing. He who had named light and sky, sun and moon, male and female, the very same God of Abraham, Isaac and Jacob whispered my name one hot July day as I overlooked a lake in northern Ohio.

Jen.

I was sixteen—

And God is as close as this story.

A Prodigal's Tale

More than twenty years ago, God said my name, and I presumed to recognize his voice. He asked me three questions, and I remember them as insistent curiosities rolling like waves and breaking gently against my prodigal life. Thinking it strange to be questioned by God, I would later learn that this is God's way. He meets and unmasks with questions.

Where are you headed?

What do you want?

Will you follow?

The kind of debauchery which, for most, requires the better part of a decade or, at the very least, a four-year university experience, I accomplished between the ages of fourteen and sixteen. More than once I had ended up drunk in unfamiliar places and unfamiliar arms. More than once I had stumbled through the front door after curfew to meet the stony face of my father. Too young to buy cigarettes, I had regrets free of charge.

Where are you headed?

> Too young to buy cigarettes, I had regrets free of charge.

I grew up in a pew. As a little girl, I used to wonder when my dangling legs would stretch long enough to touch the floor. I was six when I learned to sing from a hymnal, seven when I knelt with my mother beside my bed and prayed to ask Jesus to be my Savior. I meant those words. Several years later I was baptized. But at the age of thirteen, when our family moved to another state, I grew out of sermons and hymns, pews and crinkled Sunday school papers— much like a little girl grows out of her tap shoes.

What you do you want?

I planned for my prodigal return much later—at thirty maybe, when the sum total of adult obligations would tether me to the conditions of a holy life. I greeted repentance like a ship on the horizon of the future and believed I could sovereignly determine its anchoring. But the prodigal return came earlier than projected —at sixteen, at summer camp. It sounds terrifically cliché, but I don't suppose any of us decides our come-to-Jesus moment. We don't get to plan our Damascus road conversions.

Will you follow?

Yes.

I said yes to Jesus, got saved, if you will, by good Baptist standards, assuming, of course, that the earlier prayer by my bedside didn't take. It was a conversion rather spectacular by high school standards, especially when I stopped sleeping with my boyfriend. My friends were soon calling me "Church Lady," and even I stood astounded at the changes that happened inwardly. Jesus was palpably close, prayer honest and real. These were my new, consoling realities. Still, I couldn't shake an apprehension that strangled.

I would let go and fall far from the rescue of grace.

The nightmares began. If the beasts of temptation could be tamed in the daylight (my boyfriend and I managed to date another year with no more intimacy than a kiss), they stalked my subconscious at night,

> *We don't get to plan our Damascus road conversions.*

as lurid scenes played behind my eyes. Hell was scared out of me. And unwilling to risk my chances of recidivism, I learned quickly to do whatever it took to keep my White Knight Jesus from disappearing.

Promises.

I made promises to mute and mistrust anything that fell outside the bounds of my carefully defined categories of good. I stripped from my vocabulary the language of desire. It was, of course, what I had to blame for all the trouble I had gotten myself into in the first place.

Get thee to a nunnery.

Missionary Misadventure

In college, a team of five of us traveled for an eight-week mission trip to the southern edge of the Sahara where the road, quite literally, ended. We were not far from the fabled city of Timbuktu, a city we all knew to mean the edge of civilization. In the concrete brick house where we would spend our summer, the days were swallowed in the heat of the African sun and the never-ending job of fetching water. We were the guests of an African doctor and his wife, both well-educated Ghanaians. They had relinquished career, leaving behind even their small children, to assume their medical mission work in Mali. They were the heroes.

Every morning, we would gather in the courtyard. Seated on wooden benches and shaded by a thatched canopy overhead, we huddled around the missionary doctor, who would settle his glasses on his nose and open his Bible. Every morning, day after day, we would hear it preached in one form or another: *Suffer for Jesus' sake.* We would absorb those words so deeply into our psyches that one night, when I lay awake beside my teammate who tossed in her sleep, I heard her murmuring into the humid night air, "Suffer for Jesus' sake, suffer for Jesus' sake."

I was beginning to confidently believe that the only way of discerning what God wanted me to do was, in every case, to find the path that seemed least desirable and most difficult. There and only there could I be assured to find God's will. Surrender would always be hard; obedience would always feel grueling. Was it not Jesus, who told his disciples plainly, "Whoever wants to be my disciple must deny themselves and take up their cross daily and follow me" (Luke 9:23 NIV)? It was easy to conclude that desire was an impediment to faith, a detour from holiness. The trap of self-interest.

Impromptu Scenes

It's not yet 6 a.m., and I am ticking my lists, remembering what it is I cannot forget to do, wondering just how it is that I will get it all done. I add mayonnaise to the mental grocery list and feel life breathe hard and hot on my neck. I am the mother of five young children who has spent the last twelve years meeting life with a fair amount of grit and efficiency, building for myself the impenetrable reputation of getting things done. Five babies, putting a husband through graduate school, a short season of homeschooling, all while clinging wildly to the desire to write: the responsibilities have heaped like piles of laundry and sat heavy on my chest while the sun sleeps.

Are they all yours?

After twin boys were added to our family six years ago, strangers began stopping to ask us this question. Even now, they count the straggling parade of kids—one, two, three, four, FIVE? Their eyes widen.

How old are you?

Without proper introduction, these strangers are giving me the once-over, as if I have just paid them two dollars at the county fair to guess my age. I begin pointing to grey hairs and patting the parts of my body that jiggle, assuring them that indeed I am almost forty.

Was this planned?

That's another story altogether, one I don't usually retell as I stand in line waiting to pay for my groceries.

We are the family who has given away the crib, the car seat, and all of our fat-handled silverware. Enthusiastically, we are ridding our house of the remnants of babyhood. Our three young children, six, four and three, are meeting their milestones: the youngest is potty-trained, the oldest has just finished kindergarten. That summer, we take our first family trip to Disney World. In the fall, I plan to go back to graduate school. But the fatigue and nausea I pick up in Disney lingers on in the weeks after our return.

I should have suspected something more than the unbearable Florida heat when I began refusing my ritual cup of morning coffee. I might have wondered why, every afternoon in Disney, I routinely collapsed with the children in our hotel room, sleeping with them until almost dinnertime.

In July I learn that I am pregnant. And meet this news with no celebratory cheer, no whoop of joy, no ecstatic shout of praise. I am sullen and silent. For several weeks, I walk past my Bible in the mornings, pick up the paper instead. I cannot pray. I am not grateful. I despise that I have been treated like a token on a Monopoly board. *Do not pass go. Do not collect 200 dollars.*

How do I admit—to anyone—the crushing disappointment this pregnancy is to me? How do I reconcile the numbing depression I feel with what I know to be ultimately true about children—that they are a blessing?

I commiserate how quickly my body begins to change. "There have got to be two in there!" I tell my husband at seven weeks, eight weeks, watching with shocked horror as my belly distends almost immediately upon the surprise news that I am pregnant. "There have got to be two in there!" I tell my doctor at my first office visit, but he paternally pats my arm, breaking to me the rather obvious news that this is my fourth baby.

"You will be getting bigger earlier," he reassures, although not before agreeing to schedule an ultrasound to soothe my panicked nerves.

The day of the appointment, I leave my children at a friend's house and arrive at the hospital irritable and water-logged. Finally, I am called back into a darkened room and, once inside, dutifully settle myself onto the table. (I've done this before.) As the first image registers, the technician smiles broadly.

"Is this your first ultrasound?" she asks, the screen's image visible only to her.

"Uh-huh," I murmur unenthusiastically.

"Do you have other children?"

"Three, actually."

The quick and routine appointment I have imagined turns out to be neither quick nor routine. The technician plods along like a child distracted by the day's butterflies and ant brigades. She takes painstakingly slow measurements, waving the wand back and forth, railroading my distended abdomen, and stopping occasionally to apply pressure, which inevitably increases my discomfort and the need to pee. Her thoroughness is thoroughly unappreciated.

She never stops grinning. I watch and wonder. Does she share in the secret joys of embryonic creation? Has she plunged beneath the surface of the ordinary to find a hidden trove of miracle? I want sympathetically to understand that marvel cannot be hurried, but I am seized by the suspicion that she has been needlessly sizing not just a baby but all of my internal organs. *Hurry up*, I silently scream.

"It will only be another couple of minutes," she reassures. "Then you'll get to see your babies soon."

Babies? Babies soon. Baby soon?

We didn't plan to have five children. In truth, there have been many godless moments of these past twelve years where I have coveted a quieter life, the one where I'd be bookish and my house kept its order beyond breakfast. My own coming of age as a mother has not always been as easy and as smooth as the seamless transition many of my friends seemed to have made.

It is also true that the book I read and treasured most from my early childhood was a Little Golden Book titled *My Little Mommy*. The golden-haired girl feeds her dolls their breakfast, wipes handprints from the door frames and sets up tea parties in the backyard. Her husband is Bobby, and he drives a shiny blue car to work every morning. A thousand times I would read that book, picturing myself as that golden-haired girl who tucked her babies into bed every night.

This is my house, and I am the mommy. My children are Annabelle, Betsy and Bonnie.

Pleasures of Wordplay

Except for my brief flirtation with archaeology, I have always wanted to be a writer. As a little girl, I was adrift in questions and clinging to words, owing my love affair with words first to my father, the poet, playwright and professor who raised me to love the fun of wordplay. It was his idea of amusement to compose impromptu speeches with the words he would solicit from his children.

"Give me a word, any word. I'll talk about it for two minutes."

One day, thinking unusually hard, I searched for a word to stump my father.

"Butter."

Who knew that two minutes were so easily filled with the essential qualities of butter?

Loving words, I have always cherished books. Books have been companions all my life. As a child, whatever book I read, I seemed to reflexively choose for its company. Books have long been my certainty, words the instinctual way I puzzle out the world. They are the tools I take to my mysteries, as if by them I can carve up who I am and where in this big world I find myself.

I want to write. I am also a fixed point in my spinning sphere of domesticity. There are lunches to pack, dinners to plan, socks to pair. There are carpool obligations and clarinet lessons. My pressing responsibilities as wife and mother will not be ignored. Neither, however, will the petulance of writing be eternally put off. Like Madeleine L'Engle, who reflects in *Circle of Quiet* about the inevitable tug-of-war between her artistic life and her domestic one, I feel fragmented between my two lives, torn by a reflexive self-recrimination when I want, even need, to create space for the quiet work of reading and writing.

"I went through spasms of guilt because I spent so much time writing," writes L'Engle, "because I wasn't like a good New England housewife and mother. When I scrubbed the kitchen floor, the family cheered. I couldn't make decent pie crust. I always managed to get something red in with the white laundry in the washing machine, so that everybody wore streaky pink underwear."[1]

A year ago, our family rented an apartment in Montreal for the month of July in order to practice our French. I had also enrolled the children in a day camp for the first two weeks of our stay so that I could have some intensive time to work on this book, which back then, existed only in proposal form. After dropping them off early (and leaving our youngest in a fit of sobs), I arrived early at Blanc de Blanc every day, the neighborhood's laundromat/café. I wrote for hours, interrupting the thread of concentrated focus only to order lunch: "*pizza à la sauce Provençale avec oignons et épinards.*" At the end of two weeks, I had the majority of a book proposal completed, and it was an extraordinary sense of accomplishment—muted, however, every time my mother called to asked how the kids were enjoying "day care."

Holy Hesitations

As a mother with the will to write, I am plagued by self-doubt. Is this work I do career? Is it hobby? Is it calling? I am driven to define what I am doing in an effort to categorize it, to label it, to locate it on the map of good and bad, selfless and selfish. But I've realized that my efforts meet and challenge this theology of desire with which I've been stuck since my earliest days as a Christian, and I can't help but ask: am I really wrong to write because I want to?

Is it true that the hardest, least desirable choice is the most obviously holy? Is it true that personal desire must never be trusted? Am I right to immediately incriminate ambition?

I am a woman who has struggled long with an inordinate fear of her selfishness, a woman who has wanted a measure of certainty for finding and following the will of God. I've needed a greater reassurance that if I ever lean into my desires, I am not actually falling off a cliff.

Many, like me, imagine desire and faith in a boxing ring, facing off like opponents. We don't suppose both can be cheered at the same time. At the end of the day, one will be left standing. The other will fall. We easily dismiss desire, arguing that the goal of the Christian life is obedience. Why promote desire? Doesn't that necessarily put us in the path of potential treachery? As my friend observed when I told her I was writing a book about a theology of desire, we're apt to wonder, "Theology of desire? But isn't that an oxymoron?"

Twenty years ago, as a newly reformed sixteen-year-old who had just spent prom night playing house, I had reasons for mistrusting desire. But teen pregnancy wasn't my only reason for holding desire at arm's

> *We easily dismiss desire, arguing that the goal of the Christian life is obedience.*

length. Didn't desire keep Christians from the radical sacrifice required for following Jesus? Weren't missionaries and their commitment to total relinquishment an example we all must follow? I surmised from my time as a college student in Africa that the harder and more undesirable life was, the more eternally worthwhile and valuable. Following Jesus should be arduous, and difficulty was like a prophylactic against selfishness.

These hesitations about desire are particular to my story, but they represent a common struggle for many Christians. One doesn't have to be a mother or a writer or even a converted reprobate to recognize the inherent tensions of desire. How do we ever know when desire isn't the apple of self-actualizing promise leading us far from God? Can it ever be possible to trust our own hearts?

The first catastrophic story of human rebellion against God was, as an example, a case of wanting gone wrong. "So when the woman saw that the tree was good for food, and that it was a delight to the eyes, and that the tree was to be *desired* to make one wise, she took of its fruit and ate" (Genesis 3:6). Adam and Eve had all they could have ever needed, and yet it ceased to satisfy them. They reached past God's blessings and held out their hands for forbidden fruit. Shouldn't this serve as a lesson to all of us about the dangers of desire?

> Not only do we want what God has forbidden: we also want to be God.

Not only do we want what God has forbidden: we also want to be God. Eve was persuaded to disobey God when the serpent convinced her that she could be like God, knowing good and evil (v. 5). He called into question God's prohibition to eat from the tree of the knowledge of good and evil: "You will not surely die" (v. 4). The serpent affirmed the goodness of Eve's self-sovereignty. He heralded the wisdom by which she could rule her own life. What need had she of God? Why not do as she pleased?

We have good reasons for giving up on this business of want. As the third chapter of Genesis reveals, the pitfalls are real and our wariness warranted. There are forces around us, willing us to wring all the goodness we can out of life apart from God. Like Eve and like Adam, we enjoy listening to them. It is easy, all too easy, to arrange our lives in ways that titillate and convenience us, releasing us from the obligations of obedience and altering the exacting claims of discipleship: "If anyone would come after me, let him deny himself and take up his cross and follow me," Jesus said. "For whoever would

save his life will lose it, but whoever loses his life for my sake will
find it. For what will it profit a man if he gains the whole world and
forfeits his soul?" (Matthew 16:24-26). We are right to ask:

What can it profit a woman to want?

Shadow of a Sword

"Why does everyone need to go to India to find herself?" my friend
wants to know.

She refers to the best-selling memoir I've just finished, a story
vastly different than my own and not one I commend as orthodoxy.
The writer is a pantheist and makes her spiritual journey through
the practices of yoga and meditation, which she learns during her
stay at an Indian ashram and an apprenticeship with a Balinese
witch doctor.

Her spiritual experiences fall far outside the bounds of evangelical Christianity, and her dual search for God and pleasure (Italy
being the first stop on the road to self-discovery) begins, to my
chagrin, with an interminable and messy divorce. She and her
husband of six years had been fighting about many things, not the
least of which was whether or not to have a child. The author did
not want this. *It.* The baby, I mean. She had met her thirtieth
birthday with the knotted dread that motherhood and its imposed
sacrifices were lurking around life's next corner.

I met thirty swollen with my *third* child.

Galaxies of doctrinal space and other obvious dissimilarities
stand between this divorcée shirking motherhood as if it were an
infectious disease, and me, the woman people approach incredu-
lously at the grocery store to ask the question—"Are they *all* yours?"

But her memoir is devoted to a question I find interesting: is it
possible to be fully alive to the world of pleasure and at the same
time remain fully devoted to God? The first section records the
four months the author spends in Rome in her pursuit of pleasure.
There is pasta and wine and twenty-three pounds to show for her

successful initiation into the world of decadent living. Four months she ignores her practices of meditation, but in her estimation, it's four good months of healing from heartbreak and chronic depression. Like a beast freed from its burden and roaming at will to accept any of the world's endless invitations, she throws off her yoke of accumulated responsibilities and leaves home to find happiness.

The author shares her own wrestle with self-doubt and fears of selfishness. Her husband had accused her of selfishly wanting their marriage to end. She had recriminated herself for not wanting to bear children. "I hadn't even had the babies yet, and I was already neglecting them, already choosing myself over them. I was already a bad mother."[2] I suppose if it's true, as Virginia Woolf has said, that the shadow of the sword falls across a woman's life, this author had comfortably stepped beyond it.

Like the story of this memoir writer, the literary examples of women tangled in the tension between happiness and holiness are many: Anna Karenina falls in love with Vronsky and divorces her husband. She never realizes her happiness and eventually commits suicide by throwing herself in front of a train. Emma Bovary is bored with her husband and life in the country. She has multiple affairs, all ending badly, and poisons herself, dying a slow and agonizing death. Lily Bart, the beautiful, unmarried protagonist of Edith Wharton's novel *House of Mirth,* once compared herself to another woman—"She likes being good, and I like being happy."[3] Bart pursues a marriageable match with a wealthy man, only to die penniless and alone. We read these as the cautionary tales of desire.

Measure of Virtue

I have wanted to believe that desire is bad, that I am bad for wanting. *Suffer for Jesus' sake.* But this I can now admit: this has not always been the heroism I once thought. Often, it has been a damnable project of self-salvation.

At the core of every project of self-salvation is the staunch unwillingness to believe that God's love and forgiveness can be unmerited. Those who would try and save themselves prefer work to rest, effort to gift. Instead of receiving the free gift of grace, they wear themselves out trying to earn what has been given in Christ. They will insist upon working for the goodness they receive from God. It produces the sweat equity of works-righteousness: the wages of death (see Romans 6:23).

We are each bred with this common resistance to grace. It is never easy to live as the indebted. Kant was an eighteenth-century philosopher who extolled work as more virtuous than rest or leisure. "According to Kant, the moral law by definition is opposed to natural inclination. It is simply part of the nature of things that the Good is difficult and that the voluntary effort put into forcing oneself to do something becomes the standard for moral goodness. The more difficult thing must be the higher Good," writes German philosopher Josef Pieper, in summary of Kantian thought.[4]

To Kant, then, I might owe some of my hesitations about desire. Like Kant, I have been enamored by the moral goodness of work. It's been a longstanding love affair with striving, with effort. And because I love work, I need to insist that desire must necessarily be wrong on the basis that is it easy and something to which I am naturally inclined. I shouldn't allow myself to do and to have the things I want because that wouldn't be difficult enough to be virtuous.

Thomas Aquinas, a philosopher who lived long before Kant, could have rescued me from this misunderstanding of desire, which has no clear biblical basis. "The essence of virtue consists more in the Good than in the Difficult," wrote Aquinas. Pieper makes the distinction between Aquinas's thought and Kant's:

> The Middle Ages had something to say about virtue that will be hard for us, fellow countrymen of Kant, to understand. And what was this? That virtue makes it possible for us . . .

to master our natural inclinations? No. *That* is what Kant would have said, and we all might be ready to agree. What Thomas says, instead, is that virtue perfects us so that we can *follow* our natural inclinations in the right way. Yes, the highest realizations of moral goodness are known to be such precisely in this: that they take place *effortlessly* because it is of their essence to arise from love.[5]

Aquinas did not suggest, as Kant may have, that we overcome our natural inclinations (desires) in order to be virtuous. He illustrated that virtue, by definition, could be measured by the degree to which our desires inclined themselves toward good.

According to Aquinas, effort may not be the best measure of virtue. We aren't necessarily doing best when striving most. In fact, when it becomes more and more effortless to do all the difficult things God requires of us (love our enemies, lay down our freedoms, give generously), this may be the truest measure of our spiritual transformation. When we love and give and serve without reluctance or resentment, pride and self-congratulatory impulses, when we delight in doing the will of God (and feel less and less oppositional pull), this increasing "effortlessness" indicates a growing congruence between our desires and God's. God is at work in us, "both to will and to work for his good pleasure" (Philippians 2:13). Our desires are being transformed—and we are being formed into Christ. Coming easier to our obedience means coming into holiness.

> *Coming easier to our obedience means coming into holiness.*

Re-formation: *Sola Gratia*

We simply can't ignore desire. Like a heartbeat, desire pulses steadily in the backdrop of our lives. We may not always be aware of the work desire is doing, and yet it provides much of the necessary energy on which we rely. We get out of bed, go to work, get to the gym, marry (or not), have babies (or not), write books—follow Jesus—because in some measure, we want to.

Desire is primal: to be human is to want. Consider that wanting is the earliest language we learn. As infants, when we're yet incapable of forming words on our tongue, we're infinitely good at knowing what we want—and, for that matter, getting it. And if desire is as innate as I describe, it means that wanting, as part of the human experience, is not to be rejected but embraced. I don't mean to say that we should model our lives of wanting on the red-faced screaming

> *Desire is primal: to be human is to want.*

of a baby who's hungry, needs her diaper changed or has lost her pacifier, which her mother, on the basis of principle, refuses to retrieve. There are better ways of communicating and healthier means of expression.

The gospel of Jesus Christ meets our holy hesitations about desire, without eliminating the tension or minimizing the dangers, yet suggesting it can be reformed. Though we can indeed want in ways that go tragically wrong, in the words of the apostle Paul, we are "buried with [Christ] by baptism into death, in order that, just as Christ was raised from the dead by the glory of the Father, we too might walk in newness of life" (Romans 6:4). Might not this newness of life include a newness of desire?

The renewal of our desires is indeed the bold promise of the new covenant: the law of God will be written on our hearts (see Jeremiah 31:33), and we will *want* God. What the Mosaic law was powerless to do—to change the human heart—the new covenant, poured out for us in the blood of Christ, will achieve. It will finally grant us a real and obedient willingness to be God's people. "I will give them one heart, and a new spirit I will put within them," God promised the prophet Ezekiel. "I will remove the heart of stone from their flesh and give them a heart of flesh, that they may walk in my statutes and keep my rules and obey them. And they shall be my people, and I will be their God" (Ezekiel 11:19-20).

Before the Israelites entered the Promise Land after their forty years of wilderness wandering, Moses stood before them and renewed their covenant with God. He read aloud the law and reminded the people of their duty to obey this God who had delivered them out of slavery. "We will hear and do it," was their full-hearted response to the law (Deuteronomy 5:27). Loudly, energetically, the people of Israel declared that they would be God's people—in heart, soul, mind and strength.

But no sooner than Moses' successor Joshua had died, and the elders of his generation had died too, were the people reneging on their promises. Is it any wonder that God had groaned for their faithfulness long before their rebellion: "Oh, that their hearts would be inclined to fear me and to keep all my commands always!" (Deuteronomy 5:29 NIV). God had foreseen the sin of his people and the suffering their sin would produce. He longed for the transformation of their hearts' desires.

But no matter his goodness to them, no matter how many times he forgave their sin, the people of Israel were forever a wandering people, "a people laden with iniquity, offspring of evildoers, children who deal corruptly!" bemoaned the prophet Isaiah in the face of exile, undone by the treachery of his own people (Isaiah 1:4). "O LORD, why do you make us wander from your ways and harden our heart, so that we fear you not?" Isaiah cried aloud (63:17). He was praying for the rescue of Israel. God, save us from our wandering desires! Lord, redeem us from our impulse to leave you and love another! Make us faithful, Father!

And like all prayers that beseech the mercy of God, that prayer for rescue was finally and fully answered in the form of the Suffering Servant, whom God sent, Jesus Christ: "All we like sheep have gone astray; we have turned—every one—to his own way; and the LORD has laid on him the iniquity of us all" (Isaiah 53:6). Jesus Christ was wounded for our faithless desires. He was crushed for our wandering affections. And upon him was the punishment for every heart of stone. We—even our desires—are saved because he was bruised.

And God is as close as this story.

❧

Let there be light. God speaks, and the world illuminates, birthing a prince and a planet. He blesses them. These are the words of divine desire, our great Creator at his canvas. Every word is a brushstroke. He calls into being the world because he *wants to.* Desire is the good and beautiful momentum behind the artistry of Genesis 1. *Let there be light.* No compelling obligation stands behind these words, no shrugging sense of duty, only the heartbeat of heaven and the desire of God for humanity.

But we do not attend the words of God long. We cannot hold ourselves to heeding his words, hell-bent as we are on another voice. *Did God really say?* In some small garden long ago, a coup is mounted against the words of God.

I am Adam.

But the God of the canvas, the God of the planet and of the prince, does not and cannot relent the words of his wooing. His Son, too, is hell-bent, and the Father takes for himself a people, willing to bless them and make them his.

I, too, am Abraham.

Jen.

I was sixteen.

❧

Reflection Questions

At the end of each chapter, you are invited to reflect more personally on the ideas the author explores. Consider writing your thoughts in a journal—and then sharing them with a trusted friend.

1. Do you allow yourself to want? Why or why not?

2. When has your obedience to Christ felt most difficult and most effortless? What made the difference?

3. How does your own story with God begin? And where is that salvation now taking you?

2

Aperture of the Heart

Courage

It's a summer morning, and our task is to sort through the closet where the school uniforms hang. After breakfast, the children are stripped to their underwear, and I hand them shirts and pants, skirts and shorts. Finding pairs of last year's socks with black and threadbare soles, I hold them up as evidence. *Who's been playing in the driveway without shoes?* My owl eyes coerce no confessions.

After I have inventoried what fits, what can be handed down and what remains within the range of respectability, we pile into the car. Ten minutes later, our brood of five noisy children arrives to the visible consternation of the manager and host of college help at the uniform store. We are instantly surrounded. The three older children are whisked to the dressing rooms. The store manager then offers up one reluctant employee to "take the little ones outside to play," referring to my four-year-old twin boys who are now running in circles around the store, wearing between them the bulk of the store's headband inventory.

The pony circus stops mid-show. Realizing that this woman has just suggested they leave the store in the care of a perfect stranger, Colin and Andrew claw my legs, terrified. They will not budge. They cannot be cajoled. Finally, the manager pulls from behind the counter a large jar of plastic dinosaurs and suckers.

They fail to notice when she confiscates the headbands.

Hours later, I kick open the back door with a bang. My arms are heavy with the morning loot of school supplies, uniforms, even the groceries I've managed to pick up on our way home. I head downstairs, and a landscape of litter greets me: Legos, trains, scattered paper, headless markers. Summer's detritus of uninterrupted play is strewn about, as if someone has waited for Cinderella to appear with her broom, happily humming a tune.

I don't sing. I feel weariness hang like damp weather. I am tired—tired after our morning errands and this endless corralling of children. I am tired of summer travel and Toronto tourists. I am tired because I have five children, and they will soon be hungry for lunch. There's ice cream melting at my feet.

These are the overwhelming responsibilities of an otherwise ordinary day. And for a few more moments, I am keeping my cool, determined that melting ice cream and school uniforms will not this day start fires. I unload the groceries. Keep calm. Stay sensible. Silence the simmering tirades that I don't dare start rehearsing.

Minutes later, Nathan, our oldest son, appointed as lunch helper, can't find the mayonnaise. He calls my name absently from the kitchen upstairs.

Mom?

Hearing no reply, he calls again.

Mom?

Mom?

He's growing more insistent.

What?

I've been answering from the back of the basement every time he has called, and the echo of our voices is an irritable crescendo.

Mom?

What? I answer again, louder this time.

Moooooom?

Whaaaaaat?

Suddenly, like a sprinter out of the blocks, I am hurdling the groceries, dashing upstairs, stomping wildly with explosive rage, and I yell as soon as I have Nathan within arms' reach.

NATHAN! NATHAN! NAAAAATHAAAN!

You need to learn to come and find me instead of SCREAMING MY NAAAAME!

Which is of course the crime I now find myself committing.

Sin's Own Apologetic

I am a Christian for all sorts of reasons: because I met Jesus when I was sixteen; because my parents raised me in a Christian church; because I believe in the historical resurrection of Jesus Christ; because I find credibility in the sacred Scriptures. I am also a Christian because I think Christian theology has explosive explanatory power, especially for describing the human condition. The Christian faith tells me who I am in ways that seem most accurate to my human experience.

The Bible says that I am a sinner, not simply because I do wrong things but because I am incapable of doing better and best. The apostle Paul reminds me that "nothing good dwells within me, that is, in my flesh. For I have the desire to do what is right, but not the ability to carry it out. For I do not do the good I want, but the evil I do not want is what I keep on doing" (Romans 7:18-19). "Sin," as a biblical term, describes the haplessness of our humanity: we often do the very opposite of the good we intend. As sinners, we are superior for living in ways inferior to God's standards. We live contrary to our desires to be good and do good. Sin explains our habit of falling perennially short of our highest ideals. We sin because we do and want what is contrary to God's will. This criminality is hardly conscious much of the time.

As a mother, it's been impossible not to admit that I am a sinner. Rachel Cusk, in her book

> *"Sin," as a biblical term, describes the haplessness of our humanity: we often do the very opposite of the good we intend.*

A Life's Work, describes how "as a mother you learn what it is to be both martyr and devil," and experience yourself "as both more virtuous and more terrible, and more implicated too in the world's virtue and terror."[1]

Motherhood is exactly this petri dish where I culture the cells of my own mercurial character. One moment I'm tranquilly reading the Bible with my children at breakfast, and the next moment I'm losing my temper on account of the Hansel and Gretel crumb trail leading its way out of the pantry. Psychologically, I think they call this dissociative identity disorder. Theologically, I think we call it the split personality of sin.

I can make a million excuses for the tragedies I leave in the wake of the everyday: I'm exhausted, someone's sick, dinner must be made and someone is hungry before dinner. The pressures of motherhood, especially of the early years of sleepless nights, potty training and preschool, leave mothers feeling battle-worn. But motherhood is hard no matter what season you are in, and heroism does not recover the moment babies outgrow their diapers and board the bus for school. New freedoms surface old habits. Now that I fill much of my free time with writing, I haven't left sin behind. I've only discovered a new medium for my treachery.

My real trouble as a writer isn't trying to mean the words that I write; it's living into the words that I mean. Nonfiction writing can feel like the high art of hypocrisy, and the act of fixing words to a page can be like an inglorious act of self-crucifixion, ink indelibly driving the nails in the space that lies between life as I live it and life as I wish it were lived. *I shall not tell a lie,* said George Washington. But he was a president, not the writer of prose.

When Quentin Rowan published his first spy novel, *Assassin of Secrets,* it was initially received with glowing reviews. But five days after its release, it became clear that the novel had been almost entirely plagiarized, and the publisher immediately recalled the sixty-five hundred copies and issued an apology. Apparently, Rowan had mastered not the skill of writing a good spy novel but the mechanics of literary cut-and-paste. In her piece about Rowan for *The New Yorker,* Lizzie Widdicombe includes a paragraph from *Assassin of Secrets,* which may prove a window into Rowan's self-torturing over his many acts of hypocrisy:

> All spies are liars, it is their métier, and like ordinary liars they live in panic, knowing that the truth about themselves may be discovered at any moment—or worse, is already known by people who are too disgusted, or too clever, to confront them with it. A spy under questioning by the enemy is in a state surpassing dread because he knows that he must sooner or later tell the truth.[2]

Rowan isn't alone in living with that panic and dread. We all know a contemptible truth about ourselves. Brennan Manning was a man ordained into the Franciscan priesthood who struggled with a lifelong addiction to alcohol. He writes in *The Ragamuffin Gospel,* "Aristotle said I am a rational animal; I say I am an angel with an incredible capacity for beer."[3] Like Manning, every human is drunk on the wine of paradox and riddled with fear. We each have great capacity for evil and terrific incapacity for good.

These fears can obstruct our will to want. How can we allow ourselves to want, especially when we're so infinitely adept at sin?

> *We all know a contemptible truth about ourselves.*

How do we ever decide that our desires are anything other than the sin-sick expression of our inner corruption? Can we trust our desires if we ourselves can be so untrustworthy?

These are important questions. These are critical hesitations. And desire, if it is to be made holy, must remain committed to truth. Jesus insisted that truth is a path to freedom: "You will know the truth, and the truth will set you free" (John 8:32). Truth telling, in fact, is a way we begin in the gospel, and it is the gospel that frees our desires from fear. First, we must necessarily reject self-justification and admit the truth that we want and do wrong, committing, with damnable frequency, moral crimes and misdemeanors. But the gospel moves us beyond getting stuck in the guilt and shame of our unholy desires. We can courageously own the truth about ourselves because of the sacrificial death of God's Son, Jesus Christ: his innocence has been substituted for our guilt. Through Jesus' perfect sacrifice of atonement, truth telling becomes a means not for indictment but for acquittal.

> If we say we have no sin, we deceive ourselves, and the truth is not in us. . . . If we say we have not sinned, we make him a liar, and his word is not in us. My little children, I am writing these things to you so that you may not sin. But if anyone does sin, we have an advocate with the Father, Jesus Christ the righteous. He is the propitiation for our sins, and not for ours only but also for the sins of the whole world. (1 John 1:8, 10–2:1-2)

> *Through Jesus' perfect sacrifice of atonement, truth telling becomes a means not for indictment but for acquittal.*

We tell the truth and find our way back to grace—even the grace that permits desire.

A Challenge to the Sovereign Self

Not everyone is so quick to agree that humans are born sinners. In fact, we are assailed on every side with persuasive arguments for the goodness of humanity and the unqualified goodness of desire.

Admitting the doctrine of sin is critical to any faithful conversation about desire, not least to counter the prevailing sentiment today that everything we want is right and good. As a society, we no longer collectively subscribe to any one source of moral authority. As a result, we've generally ceded it to the sovereign self. God is dead, the church irrelevant, and in the absence of God and the church, the sovereign self has the prerogative to do as she pleases without moral restraint. She has two choices, says Nietzsche: obey or be commanded. With no one left to command, she can step over the shadow of the sword at the moment of her choosing. She can defend everything she decides to do because she has wanted to. Wanting, when the sovereign self is on the throne, is always and in every way right, and desire is the bulwark of impenetrable defense the sovereign self raises around her choices. Who will blame a person for making choices that benefit her and disadvantage others?

Of course we aren't generally so crass as to insist that we can do absolutely everything we want. A good many of us, for example, manage to remain respectable citizens despite the occasional desire to inflict bodily harm. However, I can appreciate someone like the late Christopher Hitchens, who tried to maintain a degree of continuity in his value reasoning—and perceptively illustrated when others had not.

Hitchens was a devout atheist, a man in love with liberal principles of all shapes and sizes; he was also pro-life. "I claim an absolute right to be interested in the condition of the human fetus because . . . well, I used to be one myself," Hitchens began in an essay for *Vanity Fair.*[4] Hitchens was deeply disturbed that in order to defend abortion, leftist liberals had to exchange their cherished principle of protection of the weak for the individualistic ideology of the right. Was there anyone so weak and vulnerable as the unborn child? How could liberals defend abortion on the basis of a woman's right to choose? Hitchens recognized the cult worship of the self when he saw it.

One of the most disturbing biblical portrayals we have of the social and moral disintegration that follows in the wake of self-sovereignty (and doing as we want without restraint) is the book of Judges.

The book opens at Joshua's death. The generation of the exodus is dead, along with their two most important leaders, Moses and Joshua. The first and second chapters detail Israel's failure to drive out the inhabitants from the land of Canaan despite that God had commanded them to do exactly this. God did not want his people to live among the Canaanites, for fear that proximity to a foreign people and their foreign gods would necessarily lead his people to idolatry. He was right. Cozying up to their Canaanite neighbors was exactly the disaster he had predicted. "And the people of Israel did what was evil in the sight of the Lord and served the Baals. And they abandoned the Lord, the God of their fathers, who had brought them out of the land of Egypt" (Judges 2:11-12).

A vicious cycle begins: the Israelites abandon God, they are sold by God into the hands of their enemies, and God raises up a judge to rescue them. They remain faithful to God for a generation, but the judge eventually dies and they inevitably return to their idolatrous practices—for which they are punished and rescued, again and again.

One of the last chapters of the book, chapter 19, is one of the most gruesome in all of Scripture. The chapter begins by highlighting the authority vacuum in Israel at the time: "In those days, *when there was no king in Israel*, a certain Levite was sojourning in the remote parts of the hill country of Ephraim" (v. 1). Somewhere along his travels, the Levite engages a concubine, who, for reasons that remain unclear in the text, returns to her father's house. The Levite goes to retrieve her but ends up staying several days longer because his father-in-law is strangely intent on getting him drunk and waylaying his journey.

On the fifth day, however, though most of the daylight hours have been spent in feasting and merry-making and the father-in-law again tries persuading the Levite and his daughter to spend the night, the Levite refuses. He heads into dusk with his concubine and his donkeys and eventually arrives at Gibeah, where a generous stranger takes them into his home.

The stranger warns them against staying the night in the city square, feeling they would be unsafe. Nevertheless, his worst fears for the visitors' safety are realized later that night on his very own front porch. The men of Gibeah surround the house and begin beating on the door. "Bring out the man who came into your house, that we may know him," they demand (v. 22). And they aren't just looking to make casual acquaintance.

The stranger, wanting nobly to protect his guests, offers up an ignoble alternative. "Behold, here are my virgin daughter and his concubine. Let me bring them out now. Violate them and do with them what seems good to you, but against this man do not do this outrageous thing" (v. 24). The Levite pushes his concubine out the door and locks it behind her. Safe from harm, he does nothing to intervene while her assailants "knew her and abused her all night until the morning. And as the dawn begins to break, they let her go" (v. 25). Two defenseless and innocent women are thrown to sexually rabid wolves, and it makes for an unimaginable scene of brutality and degradation. As a woman, I read the text with my blood running cold.

If the rape weren't horrid enough to convince us that something has gone terribly wrong in Israel, on its heels follows murder. The Levite opens the door the next morning only to find the concubine dead at the threshold. He tries to rouse her. "Get up, let us be going" (v. 28). When she doesn't answer, he puts her on his donkey and travels home. When he arrives home, he carves her up like a Thanksgiving turkey. Limb from limb, he dismembers her into twelve bloody pieces and sends her to the twelve tribes of Israel.

"Such a thing has never happened or been seen from the day that the people of Israel came up out of land of Egypt until his day; *consider it, take counsel, and speak*" (v. 30).

The Levite's act, in response to the violence done at Gibeah, serves as a bloody metaphor for the project of self-sovereignty. "In those days there was no king in Israel. Everyone did what was right in his own eyes" (Judges 21:25). It portrays what happens when moral restraint is cast off, human depravity unabated. When people are granted permission for doing whatever they want, it will end badly. Rape and murder are just two of the depraved inevitabilities when desire acknowledges no authority and respects no boundary.

This graphic story turns our stomachs. It poisons our imaginations. Some may wonder why it would be included in the holy canon of Scripture. My answer is this: because the Bible is the only book that will tell that kind of gruesome story. The challenge to self-sovereignty and to the unqualified goodness of desire can only be voiced when we remain committed to the most realistic view of what it means to be human. Without the doctrine of sin, we are led toward being unusually optimistic about our humanity. We will refuse to face the viciousness of our capabilities and will trust our desires too much and fear ourselves too little.

> *Without the doctrine of sin, we are led toward being unusually optimistic about our humanity.*

There are historical examples of this kind of hubris. H. G. Wells, writing before World War I, believed, as many did then, in the myth of infinite progress. "Can we doubt that presently our race will more than realize our boldest imaginations, that it will achieve unity and peace, and that our children will live in a world made more splendid and lovely than any palace or garden that we know?" Nevertheless, the horrors of bloodshed and war soon disabused Wells of his optimism: "The cold-blooded massacres of the defenseless, the return of deliberate and organized torture, mental torment, and fear to a world from which such things had seemed well nigh banished— has come near to breaking my spirit altogether. . . . 'Homo Sapiens,' as he has been pleased to call himself, is played out."[5] Keeping human sinfulness at the forefront of our minds is a moderating force in the journey of desire—even though we consider it an inconvenient truth. The doctrine of sin has the power to protect us from blind optimism, even the potential for our rescue.

Blind but Now I See

Reflecting on our desires asks us to address the more naked parts of who we are and why we do what we do. When we talk about desire, we undress our hearts. We worm our way into intention and hope to arrive at self-awareness. When we're stuck in patterns of chronic sin, we should think to ask, "What must I be wanting to continually persist in these choices?" We usually know that something is driving our behavior, but the forces often feel imperceptible to us. The simple question, "What do I want?" can lead to important change.

Recently, a new field of psychology has spawned to address this task of examining desire. Wantology, of which Arlie Russell Hochschild makes mention in her

> *The simple question, "What do I want?" can lead to important change.*

New York Times article "The Outsourced Life," is a field of expertise aimed at helping people discern their desires and work toward getting what they want. A wantologist helps clients verbalize their latent, unrequited desires and moves them toward achieving happiness by identifying the ways they can satisfy those desires. The goal of wantology is to help clients connect the dots of desire: what do they want, and how do they get it? I suppose if we are paying people to help us in this task, we're admitting both that it's difficult and that most of us lack the skills for doing it on our own.

But wantology can't offer all the answers we as Christians need. As followers of Jesus, we're asking different questions and in need of different answers. We're asking not just *What do I want?* but *Is what I want right?* We're interested in congruence: *Is what I want what God wants for me? Am I following God's will?* But this kind of reflective, prayerful examination of our heart's desires, when we're honest about it, can challenge us to see the ways we've clamored to get what we've wanted and ultimately failed to trust. It's not a truth we find easy to see. It's often a truth we'd rather avoid. Our dismissal of desire may be built less on our holy hesitations about desire. In fact, ignoring our desires may serve as the convenient way we remain ignorant and resist change.

❧

"I've been reading your blog," my friend starts after dinner as we clear plates and rinse dishes. Our children had been growing up together before we moved from Chicago to Toronto. We had attended Bible study together, traded carpool responsibilities and exchanged birthday gifts. This is the friend who had been watching my children the day I returned with the ultrasound picture of the twin babies I had been carrying only four years earlier.

> Ignoring our desires may serve as the convenient way we remain ignorant and resist change.

"I read and think, 'Yeah, that's the same old Jen.'"

I brace for support.

"You know. You write about how you're always struggling with the whole motherhood thing, how you're wanting more. You seem discontent and unsatisfied."

I nod.

"Don't you think that's actually a form of coveting?"

Sticks and stones might break your bones. And words, they gut your insides.

§

In an early chapter of *Pilgrim at Tinker Creek*, Annie Dillard recounts what she learned from stories of blind patients who recovered their sight after surgeons had learned how to safely remove cataracts.

Though we might imagine that these newly sighted people felt ecstatic, in every instance, their new capacity was disorienting. In many cases, it was even terrifying. Patients struggled to make use of their new sense, and some rejected it altogether, "continuing to go over objects with their tongues," writes Dillard, "and lapsing into apathy and despair." One patient, a fifteen-year-old boy, cried, "No, really, I can't stand it any more. . . . If things aren't altered, I'll tear my eyes out."[6]

In the Scriptures, one of the most prominent metaphors for spiritual conversion is recovering sight. When we come to a saving faith in Jesus Christ, we are healed of the spiritual blindness into which we were born (see John 9:39). This repairs our ability to see Christ as well as to see ourselves. It's this new "sight" which causes us to acknowledge both that Christ saves and that we desperately need such saving.

But like the newly sighted patients whom Dillard describes, our new sense can disorient, even terrify us. This may be owed to the theological truth that our spiritual eyes are not mere transmitters of perception. Indeed, Jesus teaches that our spiritual eyes emit light, sending up from the caverns of the self either brooding darkness or soul incandescence. "The eye is the lamp of the body. So, if your eye is healthy, your whole body will be full of light, but if your eye is bad, your whole body will be full of darkness. If then the light in you is darkness, how great is the darkness!" (Matthew 6:22-23).

It is often true that once we are made to see, we don't like what we apprehend. Spiritually seeing, we learn who we are. We recognize our heart's attachments. We see into our own heart of darkness. It should be of no surprise that when Jesus teaches about corollary health of eye and body, he does so in the context of teaching about money. "No one can serve two masters, for either he will hate the one and love the other, or he will be devoted to the one and despise the other" (v. 24). Spiritual sight gives us the frightening capacity for recognizing what we have loved and desired more than God.

Our continual challenge is to embrace this capacity for spiritual sight, which isn't just the ability to see but the willingness to *be seen*. We must be seen by God, by others, and must even will ourselves to stand naked in front of a mirror. As we see and are

> *Spiritual sight gives us the frightening capacity for recognizing what we have loved and desired more than God.*

seen, we will begin to wrestle with the nature of our desires, even find the courage to admit when they fall painfully short of God's glory. Like the cataract patients Annie Dillard describes, we may want to reject this new sense, not least because spiritual "sight" commits us to a posture of sustained humility: humility before the Scriptures as they, in Eugene Peterson's words, "read us";[7] humility in our relationships, which we injure; humility in prayer to the God before whom we are "naked and exposed" (Hebrews 4:13). Humility is one of the hardest habits to wear—which may be why talking about desire is sometimes the last thing we want to do. But we must see the truth, own the truth, tell the truth, receive the truth, live in the truth—about who we are and about what we want.

Half-truths

My husband and I were visiting a church several years ago on New Year's Eve. Halfway through the sermon, I wanted to stand and serve up my objections.

"Have you ever heard anyone pray," the pastor asked, "'God, help me to love you more?' How many of you have ever asked that of your husband or wife? Who asks their husband or wife for help like this? No, you don't go to your husband or wife and say, 'Help me to love you more.' That's your job. And when we go to God asking, 'Help me to love you more,' we're praying the wrong kind of thing. Instead, we should pray, 'Help me to *know* you more.' Because when we grow to *know* God more, when we read our Bibles and learn more about God, it will automatically be true that we will *love* God more."

These are the half-truths that imperil our faith.

We stand to recognize that there may be more to blame for our spiritual misfortunes than wrong thinking. My personal experience bears out that my head and its lack of knowledge are less to blame than my heart and its lack of love. "God, help me to love you more," is a prayer of desire, and it often feels like the only right way to pray when, despite all its proper theologies, my heart still suffers the division of its affections (see Psalm 86:11). When we pray in this way, we admit all the idolatrous impulses we cannot change on our own. We reach out to God for a healing that we cannot effect on our own.

My heart, probably like yours, is not fully set on God. I don't fully desire him or the coming of his kingdom. I consider verses like Isaiah 26:8 (NIV), "Your name and renown are the desire of our hearts," and can only admit how little that is true of my heart and how hopelessly divided I am in the manner Paul talks about in Romans 7. I, too, want what I shouldn't and fail the standards I know to be right. It doesn't matter if my morning's reading has me in James ("You have lived on earth in luxury and self-indulgence," James 5:5) or Hosea ("We will say no more, 'Our God,' to the work of our hands," Hosea 14:3), but I feel all the words penetrate and pierce someplace deep, "discerning the thoughts and intentions of [my] heart" (Hebrews 4:12). I'm a fiend, a fake.

The Bible is not just information about God: it is the living voice of God. Like a surgeon's scalpel, the Scriptures make deep incisions in my contradictions. I know to give and give away, believe and trust, but still I continue my hoarding, my doubting. As I read, I begin identifying the root of my sin problem: "No good tree bears bad fruit, nor again does a bad tree bear good fruit. . . . The good person out of the good treasure of his heart produces good, and the evil person out of his evil treasure produces evil, for out of the abundance of the heart his mouth speaks" (Luke 6:43, 45). I begin realizing I need much more profound and radical change than I had previously thought.

> *The Bible is not just information about God: it is the living voice of God.*

No, the knowing isn't always my problem. The wanting has me tangled up. For this reason, cognitive models of change, which never prod me to examine my desires or ask God to change them, have the inconsequential effect that James K. A. Smith describes in his book *Desiring the Kingdom*: "It's as if the church is pouring water on our head to put out a fire in our heart."[8] Though the church may prefer traveling the impersonal terrain of theology, it stands to recognize how wanting troubles its people: wanting too little of what God wants, wanting too

much of what the flesh demands. Paying attention to what lies beneath
the epidermis of behavior—and pursuing transformation at the level
of desire—will, however, require courageous acts of seeing.

It will also initiate grace.

He Who Sees

Come, and see a man who has seen me (see John 4:29).

The woman gathers up her skirts and runs into town, breathless
with news. She had never expected to meet anyone at the well in
the noonday heat. But this day, she had met a strange man and had
had a strange conversation. He had known the intimate details of
her life and had even seen into her bedroom.

She had no husband. This she had admitted to him. But he knew
that she'd had five husbands, referring of course to the five men
she'd slept with on the condition of their promise that they would
love her—until they each left, one after the other, abandoning her
to an empty house and all that aching, naked loneliness. The Samaritan woman was the Hester Prynne of Sychar, a woman who
kept only one companion now: shame.

The strange man saw this. He knew her story. He had read all of
its sordid chapters. And why had he made conversation with her?
He was a man and she a woman. He a Jew, she a Samaritan. He a
holy prophet, she a woman of ill repute. He'd begun the exchange
in such a strange way, making that impossible and equally irresistible invitation: living water.

"Give me this water," she pleaded (v. 15).

What was it about this man that nurtured her small, shriveled
seed of hope? Why should she ever believe a man again when
all they'd ever done was promise lies in exchange for sex? He
awakened something sleeping in her, a desire to find herself in the
arms of something—someone—so deeply satisfying that she could
drink in its abundance and nourish the arid places of self-hatred
and shame. Something made her begin believing again.

But when the man tells her to go and call her husband, she feels the relentless, unforgiving sun hanging overhead. She is undressed. "I have no husband" (v. 17).

The unscrupulous woman avoids Jesus' intimate gaze and turns the conversation instead to the hotly contested religious claims of her day: "Our fathers worshiped on this mountain, but you say that in Jerusalem is the place where people ought to worship" (v. 20).

Open shame is always a terrifying proposition. We run to avoid the truth about ourselves, the truth that is not hidden from God.

If you knew the gift of God.

The hope of the gospel echoes. We can neither undo the wrong we have done, nor can we promise to do better. Our hearts are infirm, and there is absolutely no chance that we can heal them. We will chronically want wrong things, and we will not be able to interrupt this cycle of self-destruction on our own. Instead, we have to reach out to the one who died to achieve what we could not. The gospel can end our futile games of hiding and pretending, of taking cover in all our impersonal, theological abstractions so that we avoid introspection and the gaze of God. The gospel reminds us that God has seen the worst of us and chooses, in our place, to see his Son. We have no need of exhausted methods of spiritual performance or pretension. We have no more reason to hide. And because of Jesus Christ and his willing death in our place, we have every reason to pray and have the confidence that, should we approach the throne of grace, it is mercy we will receive every time (Hebrews 4:16).

Where are you headed? What do you want? Will you follow?

Brave is she who owns her story of desire.

Admission of Guilt

> Brave is she who owns her story of desire.

When I walked into a friend's home our first summer here in Toronto, I had expected a house swarming with sticky-fingered kids and crying babies. After all, it was moms' group. But when the six of us paraded through the front door and I panned the room, there was hardly a kid in sight.

Where were all the children?

Some of the mothers had stolen away from the office for a couple of hours to attend our morning meeting. Others were on maternity leave for their second child and had kept their childcare arrangements for the first. But no one had as many children as I, and certainly no one had their children home all summer.

Suddenly, my standards for "Mom Enough" were turned on their head. Never would I find the "good" moms I knew back in Chicago sipping coffee uninterrupted in the middle of summer. In the suburban American landscape we'd left behind, "Mom Enough" had come to mean choosing domesticity over career. For the extreme moms, who loved Jesus incrementally more and willingly laid down their lives with that extra measure of heroism, they bore more children than most and kept them home for their schooling.

By these standards of "good" mom, I had qualified for my merit badge. I'd stayed home. I'd borne five children. For a short season, I had even homeschooled.

But as it turns out, I was still not "Mom Enough."

If ever I had needed proof, I had only to think about the clutch of self-loathing that would grab me by the throat every time a friend (a friend!) posted adorable pictures of her son on Facebook. When, for Mother's Day, she posted the song she'd written and recorded to celebrate his first year of life, I could not bear to listen beyond the first several bars.

The truth is, the song, the pictures, the status updates like, "My little angel, what would my life be like with you?" felt like a gavel had dropped on my own parenting. *What was wrong with me?* I treasured my children but could never write what she wrote nor feel what she felt.

Yeah, that's the same old Jen.

My friend's earlier accusation—that I had coveted—has bored holes through me. It has worked me hard for a confession. And I admitted to my friend then, as I have often enough admitted to myself and to God, I have not always found it easy to embrace the enormity of motherhood. Yes, I have envied women with fewer children (and less laundry). Yes, I have even wanted more than motherhood, even for as much as I have wanted it.

But has that struggle—of want, maybe even of coveting—cast me beyond the reach of God? Bravely, I will own this story.

Because—if you knew the gift of God.

Reflection Questions

1. How can the gospel inspire your willingness to "see and be seen"?

2. What changes are you resisting as you ignore your own desires?

3. If you bravely owned your story of desire, what longings and even disappointments would you begin admitting?

3

Precipice of Hope

Grace

I don't find him handsome at first.

We meet at an impressive school on Chicago's North Shore, the school where, by sheer providence, I have landed my first job as a high school French teacher. In advance of my interview, my husband and I drive through the shaded streets of this wealthy suburb and stare agape at the homes concealed from view by tall fences and gated driveways. We wind our way to the school and arrive to discover a profusely Ivy League landscape: buildings of brick and stone, lawns that stretch expansively. By all comparisons, I am unimpressive—twenty-two, without any real teaching experience except the six weeks I have substituted at a local middle school.

I am hired. And take this for no spectacular accomplishment. I am an unspectacularly warm body, and it's April: the school's French teacher is ballooning with a baby. I may be inexperienced, but even at twenty-two, I've managed to convince the principal that I am not likely to mess things up too terribly. Later that spring, I am rehired for the next school year. And weeks later, I get a call from the school's athletic director.

"So you've indicated here that you'd be able to coach cheerleading?" she notes, closing the door behind her on the day I have agreed to meet her in her office. It's true that I was a cheerleader in high school, even in college. It is less true that I can coach cheerleading.

I am hired.

The school year begins, and weeknights drag late. After full days of teaching, I change out of my heels, pull on a pair of running shoes and try to figure out, on the fly, how one actually coaches cheerleading. We meet. He is a teacher, too, and coaches football. This brings him down to the field everyday where the cheerleaders practice. We're seeing each other every day. Soon he's lingering longer.

It's innocent enough. I don't pay serious attention to his attentions, and I don't even really consider it attention that he grins boyishly, banters playfully, until one day at a professional development meeting my colleagues point out that he's flirting with me.

He likes you.

I am married.

By all accounts, my marriage to Ryan has begun well, and I have no intention of jeopardizing it. Our first years together are placid ones. But because we are twentysomethings who have professionally catapulted ourselves into the real world, we spend considerable time apart. Ryan, an actuary, spends his evenings and weekends poring over stacks and stacks of index cards covered in mathematical hieroglyphics. I don't see much of him. In these first years of marriage, when all the rest of our friends are tying the knot, I travel to the weddings alone.

This symbiotic solitariness is not to be blamed entirely on him. My department chair, a tired father of an energetic toddler and a lively preschooler, has warned me, *If you don't do it now, you may never do it*, and on his advice, I have begun graduate school. This, in addition to my teaching and coaching responsibilities, estranges us further.

Any dolt knows that marriages, like plants, thrive when they are nurtured. But we are not feeding ours. The casual conversations

with the handsome football coach become more frequent. I begin
noticing how good it feels, during the school day, to bump into him
at the copier. I even begin deliberately planning these encounters,
though admitting this collusion to no one, not even to myself. If it
is indiscretion, I find it proportionately small.

One night, at the end of the school year, we have ended up at a
student's graduation party together. We circulate apart for most of
the evening, but at one point, he manages to pull me aside and ask
if I want to go out later, after the party.

Yes.

I say yes.

How much times passes between the time when I accept the invitation and later decide to leave? I gather my things—but make no
obvious attempt at finding him, resisting what could be interpreted
as full complicity. I head for the front door.

(Beyond this?)

I am there. Standing at the door. Before I can turn to see if he is
following, an impatient wind gusts at my back. The door opens. I
explode into the night air. This force, this wind, it will not, it does
not, concede my hesitation. I find I am running. Breathless, panicked, I am fleeing the scene. I don't turn to look around. I don't stop.
I'm just running, running. Running. I jump into my car, slam the
door and speed home.

I wake Ryan to tell him everything.

Acts of Seizure

It was grace gusting at my back that night nearly fifteen years ago.
I knew it then, appreciate it even more profoundly now.

Grace is not only needed for the occasion of conversion, the
moment we suddenly (or slowly) come to our senses and realize
that we are spiritually bankrupt, having nothing to bring to God
and everything to receive. Grace is also required for the long
season of cultivated growth that follows that rebirth. By grace

we set out. By grace we are also sustained. Grace has as much to say about endings as it has to say about beginnings.

Like the apostle Peter, we aren't fully aware of our capacities for betrayal. No matter how much we feel stayed on Christ, we are in perpetual motion—and in need of grace. Grace is the freedom to admit our failure to be

> *Grace has as much to say about endings as it has to say about beginnings.*

linear and plot a direct course to God. Like sheep, we are given to ignorance, even outright stupidity, and grace is our homing instinct, provided for the protection we don't know that we need, ensuring that we don't ever wander too far.

My story of near-marital catastrophe (if indeed, it had been poised to become that) is not unlike the story of Lot when sulfur threatens to rain down from heaven on his hometown of Sodom. Lot is a man who, after parting ways with his uncle Abraham, moves in the direction of the Jordan Valley, "as far as Sodom" (Genesis 13:12). Lot, unlike Abraham, settles outside of the divinely prescribed boundaries of Canaan. He is lured by the promise of well-watered land. And despite what may look like an initially propitious choice, we have hint early in the text that this will not bode well for Lot. We are warned that "the men of Sodom were wicked, great sinners against the LORD" (v. 13).

Soon enough, the kings of Sodom and Gomorrah are defeated in battle, and Lot, along with his entire household and possessions, is taken captive and held until uncle Abraham comes to the rescue with his 318 trained fighters. Presumably, Lot resettles himself back in Sodom after the war, but we don't hear anything about him until several chapters later, when he re-enters the text. In Genesis 18, God announces to Abraham that he plans to destroy Sodom and Gomorrah. Abraham intercedes for the salvation of Lot and his household, and two angels are sent to Sodom on Operation Rescue. They find Lot, on the eve of the city's destruction, at the city gate.

The depravity of the city, which has merited God's wrath, is on evident display that night as the men of Sodom surround Lot's house for the purpose of raping the two guests. But these men, groping for a night of fun, are struck blind, impeded from their plans of perversion, and the following morning, as black clouds gather in the sky, the angels deliver desperate, fevered warnings of God's impending judgment on the city. "Up! Take your wife and your two daughters who are here, lest you be swept away in the punishment of the city" (Genesis 19:15). There is no time to spare. There is no time for Lot to waste words on his sons-in-law, who have taken this whole business of doom as a hoax. But Lot hesitates. He lingers. We don't know if he finds it too difficult to imagine that God's judgment can be so swift and severe. Maybe he dares to presume that his city will be spared. But God does not, God will not, give way to Lot's unholy pause.

Grace grabs hold.

"The men seized him and his wife and his two daughters by the hand, the LORD being merciful to him, and they brought him out and set him outside the city" (Genesis 19:16).

> Every act of seizure is an occasion of grace.

The Lord being merciful to him.

I am Lot.

And every act of seizure is an occasion of grace.

A Greater Work

When the Israelites were delivered from Egypt, they found themselves in the wilderness. Food and water ran in short supply, and they lamented the meals they had left behind. "They willfully put God to the test by demanding the food they craved. They spoke against God; they said, 'Can God really spread a table in the wilderness?'" (Psalm 78:18-19 NIV). The nation of Israel wanted meat. Why hadn't God given meat? He was impotent and indifferent, they accused. And God heard these bitter complaints; he heeded their impatient desires. "They ate till they were gorged—he had given them what they craved. But before they turned from what they craved, even while the food was still in their mouths, God's anger rose against them" (vv. 29-31 NIV). Men and women died that day, judged for the impertinence of their demands. They did not regard God, had only regard for their desires.

In the first chapter of Romans, we see a similar tragedy of sinful desire: men and women are given over to their "lusts" (v. 24), to "impurity" (v. 24), to the "dishonoring of their bodies" (v. 24), to "dishonorable passions" (v. 26), and to a "debased mind" (v. 28). They are men and women who refused the knowledge and honor of God, men and women who failed to live gratefully in response to their Creator. They are given up for lost, surrendered by God into the hands of their own disastrous desires. Rather than impeding their self-destruction, God stays his hand. He refuses to intervene. His wrath against their sin is demonstrated by his inaction: no longer will he persist in warning them, no longer will grace intervene. Like C. S. Lewis describes in *The Great Divorce*, they are committed to the hell of their choices. "There are only two kinds of people: those who say to God, 'Thy will be done,' and those to whom God says, in the end, '*Thy* will be done.'"[1]

I shudder to read these stories. They remind me that my greatest punishment may be the occasion of getting what I foolishly want. They remind me of my continuing need for grace, which is always actively at work to interrupt my cycles of self-destruction.

Apart from the hope of the gospel, of Jesus Christ crucified for faithless sinners, these stories would inspire paralyzing fear. And unfortunately, fear has been a well-worn path in my own spiritual journey, especially in the context of desire. I've been afraid of my own potential treachery, which, as my story reveals, seems warranted. I've run ragged with the worry that, without proper vigilance, my heart will career off course. These fears keep me from the risk of desire. How do I want when I am found wanting?

But fears like these indicate the greater work grace has yet to do in me. "Whoever fears has not been perfected in love" (1 John 4:18). Grace (the boundless, undeserved love of God for sinners) unbinds us from fear: fears of falling, fears of failing. Somehow, I had to begin trusting more fully that God had dedicated himself to the project of forming Christ in me. Yes, I would want wrong things—and God would persist in loving me still.

> *Yes, I would want wrong things—and God would persist in loving me still.*

All throughout Scripture, we're reminded that our spiritual formation isn't fully about us, as if God's end goal were to make us more holy. Our holiness is not the end, but the means toward God's ultimate goal, which is to honor his own name. "Though our iniquities testify against us, act, O LORD, for your name's sake" (Jeremiah 14:7). From the very first rescue mission God enacted for the people of Israel (their deliverance from Egypt), God asserted a purpose from which he will not eternally retreat: "I will get glory" (Exodus 14:4). God's determined pursuit of his own glory, even his glory through us, advances us beyond the fears of our troubled and restless humanity. God isn't giving up on us—because he isn't giving up on his own glory. We will be formed into the image of Christ because God has determined this from before the moment the foundations of the world were laid (see Ephesians 1:4). Our desires will be changed.

The Priority of Love

The goal of Christian formation is the slow, steady shaping of our lives into the posture and practice of love. "Love is the fulfilling of the law," wrote the apostle Paul (Romans 13:10). He remembered well that Jesus, under the scrutiny of the religious leaders, distilled the Mosaic law into two simple commands: love God and love your neighbor (see Matthew 22:34-40). Our hearts might incline themselves toward selfish desire, but the Copernican revolution of grace will move us beyond our selfish desires to Christ and to neighbor—to love, in all these forms. Love is our highest mandate—and desire critically important to our spiritual lives.

The redemption of desire is an infinitely bigger project than making sure Christians toe moral lines and recite right doctrines. Unfortunately, as the Pharisees prove, we can be virtuous and theological —without having ever loved. Straining

> God isn't giving up on us—because he isn't giving up on his own glory.

gnats and swallowing camels, the Pharisees were hyper-ethical. They were also the most scripturally well-versed men of their day. But Jesus reserves his fiercest judgment for them: "You hypocrites! Well did Isaiah prophesy of you, when he said: 'This people honors me with their lips, but their heart is far from me; in vain do they worship me, teaching as doctrines the commandments of men'" (Matthew 15:7-9). The Pharisees' moral rectitude and biblical literacy did not promote affection for God: their spiritual endeavors, like bent arrows, were aimed at the wrong target. They did not understand the priority to become lovers.

Jesus came to right what the religious leaders had turned upside down. In the incarnation, he brought love to earth, pitching his tent among sinners, healing disease and forgiving sin: "Woe to you, scribes and Pharisees, hypocrites! For you tithe mint and dill and cumin, and have neglected the weightier matters of the law: justice and mercy and faithfulness. These you ought to have done, without neglecting the others" (Matthew 23:23). Obedience is good. Faithful obedience is important. But, as Jesus reminds, observing the nit-picky commands of the law and failing to love is a devilish exchange.

How can I be made to love more faithfully, more instinctually? When my mother calls and insists on reciting the litany of her aches and pains, why can't I patiently listen? When my husband is invited for a much-needed weekend away with his friends, why can't I celebrate his departure? When my friend's book is received warmly, why do I feel sucker-punched? When my daughter begs to be tucked in at night, why must I sigh audibly, climbing the stairs reluctantly?

James K. A. Smith argues clearly that we need more than right doctrine to grow and mature as believers in Christ. Our problem isn't that we think wrongly: it's that we love wrongly. As Saint Augustine argued, because of the fall, we have inherited "disordered loves." We either love wrong things or we love them in wrong ways. Instead of loving God faithfully, we devote our affections to trifles. To use the graphic metaphor familiar to the Old Testament prophets, we play the whore. "I will go after my lovers, who give me my bread and my water, my wool and my flax, my oil and my drink" (Hosea 2:5). We seek our good in something or someone other than our eternal husband, who is God. We are *looking for love in all the wrong places.*

Every sin is a form of spiritual adultery, and this reveals that desire is at the center of our spiritual formation and transformation. We are not merely cognitive beings whose greatest need is to think rightly about God. Change is not determined merely by having the right information. This fails to explain what it means to be human.

A better philosophical anthropology than *Homo sapien* is the one Smith proposes: he argues that we are lovers—*Homo liturgicus.*[2] We orient our lives not according to our belief systems or worldview, but according to our desires. Every decision, big and small, is value-driven, and consciously or subconsciously, we are pursuing what we love and value. "We are teleological creatures. We are the sorts of animals whose love is aimed at different ends or goals (Greek: *teloi*).

. . . Rather than being pushed by beliefs, we are pulled by a *telos* we desire," writes Smith.[3] Desire is the powerful subtext of our lives. It determines our decisions. This is why we need to pay attention to it. If we are to change, desire must change.

> *Desire is the powerful subtext of our lives. It determines our decisions. This is why we need to pay attention to it.*

To understand ourselves as *Homo liturgicus* is to say desire is a lever that moves our behavior in a visceral way. Love, as lovers know, is hardly a rational response to a set of objective data. Love, at least initially, is the stomach's thrilling, tangled, wobbly, inside-out feeling when your lover walks through the door or looks your way. Though love isn't merely a feeling, it certainly exists on more than a cerebral plane of behavior. And research shows that 40 percent of our life is lived at the level of gut reaction: we are lovers acting on instinct. Because this is true, cognitive reprogramming for the purpose of spiritual formation won't work. We have to reach deeper into the places where desire lies dormant. To effect real and lasting change, we will have to be oriented toward better desires, even toward grace. We will need transformation of the *kardia*.

English translators define *kardia* as either "heart" or "mind," but the Greek word actually encompasses both. Its best translation may be "gut." *Kardia* is the biblical word that captures both a person's rational and irrational processes, her mental and moral activity. The *kardia* must be the locus of spiritual formation if we want to experience change at the level of desire. "You delight in truth in the inward being, and you teach me wisdom in the secret heart," writes David in a psalm of confession after his tragic moral failure. He cries out to God to reorder not just his thinking but his loves. "Create in me a clean heart, O God, and renew a right spirit within me. . . . Then I will teach transgressors your ways" (Psalm 51:6, 10, 13). Like David, we have to seek transformation at the level of *kardia*, entreating God for the renewal of our thoughts as well as our loves. Desire, in addition to knowledge, must be transformed if we are to grow into an obedient life of holy effortlessness.

Immersion

At school, at work, standing in the grocery line or sitting at a baseball game, we are implicitly taught what to love and value. The good life is pictured and imagined for us in a myriad of ways (Pinterest, of course, having a corner on this market). Our desires are being shaped and stretched, formed and kneaded like a lump of dough, right under our nose—with an iPhone in our hand. We are lured by sources of counterfeit goodness. We are lied to. We want happiness—and the world will happily define the ways and means of getting it. But these are not the voices we should heed. Christian formation will always run counter to the self-aggrandizing, self-interested direction of the world's desire, and our call is to resist conformity and seek renewal (see Romans 12:1-2). This requires transformation at the deepest dimensions of our being: the *kardia*.

But how do we reach into the *kardia*? If it operates, to some extent, subconsciously, how is it changed? Prayer is at least one way we reach the *kardia* and drive deeper into grace. If we can't think our way into grace, if we can't reorder our disordered loves, then a remaining means of mercy is prayer. Prayer is the way we bring our potential (and actual) treacheries to God. Prayer is the way we admit the change that we cannot effect.

> Prayer is the way we admit the change that we cannot effect.

Create in me a clean heart, O God: this prayer (and others like it) is one of the few weapons we wield in a battle that wages invisibly for desire. "For we do not wrestle against flesh and blood, but against the rulers, against the authorities, against the cosmic powers over this present darkness, against the spiritual forces of evil in the heavenly places. . . . [Pray] at all times in the Spirit, with all prayer and supplication" (Ephesians 6:12, 18). The apostle Paul recognized the fight for our formation and the battle for our desires. As Smith puts it, there are those who "unwittingly make us disciples of rival kings and patriotic citizens of rival kingdoms."[4] As one means of resistance, Paul commended to the church the practice of prayer.

The Lord's Prayer, a prayer that Jesus taught his own disciples to pray, apprentices us in the vocation of following him. It is a lexicon of holy desire and a project of counterformation. It is not a formula of petition, not a method for getting what we want from God. In the words of N. T. Wright, "When Jesus gave his disciples this prayer, he was giving them part of his own breath, his own life, his own prayer. The prayer is actually a distillation of his own sense of vocation, his own understanding of his Father's purposes."[5] The prayer is uniquely reflective of Jesus' self-understanding: who he is and what he came to accomplish. By entering into the cadence of these words, we actually begin moving to the beat of his music. We learn to love what God loves and to make his desires our own. Teach us to pray, Jesus' disciples asked.

And teach me to want.

There is something very elemental about "Our Father," and the church has long seemed to recognize the Lord's Prayer as a prayer simple enough to teach our children as well as profound enough to spend a lifetime learning to mean. Many church traditions pray this prayer on every occasion of their gathering. Although some would argue that this becomes a rote recitation, I consider it an immersive experience. The language of the Lord's Prayer baptizes us into new realities. We pray this prayer again and again and we learn to see the world, ourselves, even God himself more accurately.

Before we moved to Toronto two years ago, we had decided to send our children to a bilingual school. We wanted them to learn French, and they have proven their capacity for the challenge. Recently I drove the children to school and marveled at their progress, especially when my daughter piped up from the backseat to recite the lines of her newly assigned poem:

> Aucun doute,
> C'est un mammouth;
> C'est un animal,
> Colossal.
> Mort and congelé
> Depuis une éternité.
>
> *No doubt,*
> *It's a mammoth;*

A colossal animal.
Dead and frozen
For an eternity.

Our children's success is owed, in large part, to the commitment the
school makes to an immersion experience. New students, from the
very first day of school, are addressed in French, and with a great deal
of creativity and compassion, teachers succeed in communicating
with the children. By November of that first year, I noticed that my
children's capacity for understanding French was quite strong. By
Christmas break, they were stringing together two- and three-word
phrases. By spring break, these phrases had become sentences, and by
the end of June, they were, at least in some sense of the word, "fluent."

The fluency of holy desire can be learned: it can even be learned
by praying the Lord's Prayer again and again—although, to what
may be our surprise, the Lord's Prayer doesn't levitate us into some
divine dimension where earthly concerns cease to matter. The
Lord's Prayer is a prayer for us, here and now. It teaches us to re-
enter our lives with a greater allegiance to Christ and his kingdom
while allowing us to pray for everyday, earthly desires.

To borrow from Dietrich Bonhoeffer, the Lord's Prayer is our "yes
to God's earth."[6] The Lord's Prayer is incarnational in the same way
that Jesus is incarnational. It teaches us what it means to be fully
human and pictures for us the good life. To pray it again and again
is to imbibe the holy *teloi* of God. But that plunge into holy desire
doesn't remove us from earthly life; it implicates us, gets us busy in
the business of loving and worshiping God in our neighborhoods
and churches and cities.

"Delight yourself in the LORD, and he will give you the desires of
your heart," writes the psalmist (Psalm 37:4 NIV). And as we pray the
words Jesus taught us to pray—*Our Father in heaven, hallowed by your
name*—immersing ourselves in Jesus' language, our hearts realign
with God's purposes and priorities. Then, as the psalmist writes, we

discover that our desires are *given* by God—not in the sense of granted, but more in the sense of confided. Holy prayers of desire don't simply aim to get something from God: they're ambitious to get God in us.

Lead Us Not

The Lord's Prayer, like all prayer, is part work and part rest. Perhaps the only work we do is getting ourselves

> *Holy prayers of desire don't simply aim to get something from God: they're ambitious to get God in us.*

there. Once we've gotten ourselves there—to prayer—whatever remains of productivity is God's job. As I recently read Mary Karr's third memoir, *Lit,* I was reminded that no sincere prayer could be considered bad prayer. Misguided? Yes. Self-interested? Yes. Irreverent? Absolutely. And all of these would describe Karr's first attempts at prayer on her journey to getting sober and sane. Everyone tells her to pray, which she insists she cannot do. She doesn't even believe in God.

Her friends tell her to pray anyway.

"Yield up what scares you. Yield up what makes you want to scream and cry. Enter into that quiet. It's a cathedral," her friend says.[7]

"[But] how does getting on your knees do anything for you?" Mary asks.

"It makes you the right size."[8]

Mary finally takes up the suggestion to pray after she's checked herself into a mental hospital, having abandoned her planned suicide by which she would widow her husband and orphan her son. How many prayers, I wonder, are driven by this anguished state of soul bankruptcy? "Be gracious to me, O LORD, for I am languishing. . . . Turn, O LORD, deliver my life; save me for the sake of your steadfast love. . . . I am weary with my moaning; every night I flood my bed with tears; I drench my couch with my weeping. My eye wastes away because of grief" (Psalm 6:2, 4, 6-7). The Psalms alone are replete with examples of people that are driven to God by despair.

"In the hospital, I have this urge to kneel," Karr writes. "I tiptoe to the bathroom and bend onto the cold tiles. *Thanks, whoever the f— you are, I say, for keeping me sober.*"[9]

Can we pray profanity? Grace may be as bold to suggest that we can. And it's grace that I find in hearty measure in the Lord's Prayer.

Lead us not into temptation, but deliver us from evil.

In Matthew's Gospel, this is the concluding phrase of the Lord's Prayer. For me, it is where I want to begin in my journey of desire. *Lead us not into temptation, but deliver us from evil.* This phrase is grace itself. It presumes the paradox of being human. It acts like a vote of non-confidence. As we pray for God to spare us the test (and the word does mean testing rather than temptation), we are admitting our vulnerabilities. Here are the words that teach us to see ourselves poised on the brink of self-imposed disaster. Here are the words to remind us that our only hope is to inquire after grace. Only grace can stand between us and any of our stupid declarations of "I shall be safe, though I walk in the stubbornness of my own heart" (Deuteronomy 29:19). By praying this prayer, by admitting our weaknesses, we are daring to believe that God can care enough to deliver us, even from ourselves.

Our moral frailty is a strange consolation. "He told us to beg God not to put us to a test, presumably because we would fail it," wrote Telford Work in *Ain't Too Proud to Beg.*[10] The Lord's Prayer reminds us that there are no divine delusions about human faithfulness. God understands the human soul to be a drifter. "He knows our frame; he remembers that we are dust" (Psalm 103:14). We are moral simpletons, easily captured by ignorant desires. Like a child in a candy store, we will demand sugar with no thought of cavities. We will want wrong things. We will ask God for wrong things. And we will be angered when he refuses us.

Lead us not into temptation, but deliver us from evil. This prayer of Jesus helps us heave the burden of our ignorant human selfishness onto the shoulders of God. It is a prayer winged with hope, a prayer that carries desire to the throne of grace and makes simultaneous space for both unholy desire and rescue.

Lead us not into temptation, but deliver us from evil. God will save us—from ourselves.

God's Desire for Us

We were a ragtag band of writers: Dave, Andy, Chris, Wendy and me. We'd committed the better part of a week to our individual projects, which included entertaining stories of Mr. Lizard, the reptile who lived in a bedroom shared by two young girls. He introduced himself with a thick Indian accent as "Gecko Sahib."

I'd come to the convent and its soaring ceilings with a rough draft of questions and curiosities about desire, and over the course of that week, ideas began to formulate and take shape. I wrote relentlessly, giving myself over to a surprise torrent of words. Waking early, writing late, I kept a breathless pace and retrieved pieces of buried history.

When Thursday afternoon arrived, the flood of language slowed, and I made an appointment with a woman from a local church congregation. I was told she was gifted in intercessory prayer, and she agreed to pray for me. We met several hours later, and after perfunctory introductions, she laid her hands on my head and opened her prayer like this.

"Father, your desire is for us. You want to be with us, and it is not difficult."

Her words exploded over me like a thunderous clap of grace. I was writing

> It is never we who seek God. It is he who seeks us.

about desire—*human* desire—wrestling to understand what place my wanting had in my journey of faith. But I was suddenly reminded of what is always preeminent in the life of faith: it is never we who seek God. It is he who seeks us.

The thread of redemption running through the weave of Scripture reminds us how God commits himself to friendship with the people he has made. This is, of course, the gospel, *the good news.* Before the fall, Adam and Eve share intimacy with God. God keeps their company in the garden as they walk and talk with him. But even after the fall, God remains committed to having human companions. Noah walks with God, having found favor with him. Abraham is sought by God, and God blesses Abraham with land and family. Moses encounters the living God at the burning bush. He develops habits of conversation with God, speaking to him face to face as friends do. The Israelites are chosen from among the nations as God's treasured people and possession, "not because you were more in number than any other people . . . for you were the fewest. . . . It is because the LORD loves you and is keeping the oath that he swore to your fathers . . . Know therefore that the LORD your God is God, the faithful God who keeps covenant and steadfast love" (Deuteronomy 7:7-9).

It's often perceived that the God of the New Testament is a new and improved version of divinity, more loving than wrathful, more generous than hostile, but this intensely personal God I describe is the God of both the Old and New Testaments. The Scriptures record the long and consistent history of God's gentle ways with humanity. As he described himself to Moses, he is, "the LORD, the LORD, a God merciful and gracious, slow to anger, and abounding in steadfast love and faithfulness" (Exodus 34:6). God has always been extravagantly patient with sinners.

The forbearance and faithfulness of God were characteristics which Abraham presumed when he interceded on behalf of Sodom and Gomorrah: "Will you indeed sweep away the righteous with the wicked? . . . Far be it from you to do such a thing, to put the righteous to death with the wicked, so that the righteous fare as the wicked. Shall not the Judge of all the earth do what is just?" (Genesis 18:23, 25). Abraham prayed with a confidence in the goodness of God—even when standing face to face with the prospect of God's irrevocable and terrifying judgment.

But God doesn't reserve favors for his favorites. Divine goodness has never been predicated upon the goodness of humanity. Abraham's prayers were not heeded because he was spectacularly faithful. The last biblical scene of Noah's life ends on a sordid note. Moses is prohibited from entering the Promised Land because he'd failed to maintain God as holy before the people. And Israel? Well, we have a long record of their faithlessness.

The Bible isn't a storybook of heroes. It features ordinary actors, each of them inconsistent, unreliable. The Bible bears out God's grand and heroic story of rescue in the lives of the un-extraordinary, and redemption comes to the stage of screw-ups. These, for example, are the names that figure into the Gospel writer Matthew's genealogy of Christ:

- Abraham, liar

- Jacob, cheat

- David, adulterer and murderer

- Manasseh, most wicked of all the Israelite kings

These are the good-for-nothing ancestors of the King. And the genealogy reads exactly as it should, like a kind of neon advertisement for life with God: "Wanted: men and women who've screwed it up royally." To say that God has wanted friendship with his creation and pursued them with a persistent and everlasting love is not the same thing as saying that men and women have been worthy of that love or that God has been tolerant of their indiscretions.

But it is to say this: that God purposes good for those who, because of grace, love him and are called according to his purpose. Desire, in all of its complicated forms, is not removed from grace. There is indeed hope for selfish sinners because Christ has died, Christ is risen, and Christ will come again. This is the victory that the church has long been proclaiming over the enemies of sin and death and the disease that takes up residence, even in our own hearts.

The one who came in grace and truth—Jesus Christ—he alone faced temptation and evil and bore up under their unholy weight. At the beginning of his ministry in Matthew 4, Jesus is led into the wilderness to be tempted by the devil. Forty days and forty nights of hunger are parallel to the Israelites' forty years of wandering, and he is faithful in the ways that they were not. In Matthew 26, just moments before his arrest, Jesus falls to his knees in a garden, and it is not unlike the garden of our beginning. But he eats no apple, feeding instead on the will of his Father.

It takes him to hell and back.

Lead us not into temptation, but deliver us from evil. Unlike a prayer of moral resolution, this is our white flag of moral surrender. We face our depravity, even in the face of our desires—and we embrace *euangelion*, the good news of the first-century miracle. Jesus has exchanged death for life, love for indifference, sacrifice for selfishness, innocence for guilt, and looking back at the moment of historic exchange and his faithfulness, we learn to pray, *Lead us not into temptation but deliver us from evil.* To this prayer, Jesus joins his own faithful intercession:

> *Father, forgive them,*
> *for they know not*
> *what they want.*

Father, forgive them, for they know not what they want.

Reflection Questions

1. How does the prayer "Lead us not into temptation" help you face your own capacities for betrayal?

2. What might prevent you from believing that God's desire is for you, his grace strong enough to save?

3. Imagine God telling you, "*Thy* will be done." What would this mean?

4

Project Kingdom

Good News

We uprooted our family of seven, crossed an international border and settled in Toronto, a city where the subway rumbled under our feet in the library check-out line and buses squealed and heaved and moaned. We traded in our predictable suburban conveniences (free parking, left-hand turn lanes, drive-through Starbucks), downsized to one bathroom, gave up homeschooling and enrolled our children in a bilingual school. Like a dinghy caught in a storm, life's familiarities had capsized. We even left behind air conditioning.

Of course the easiest answer for the insanity of removing our children from all that was familiar to them was that Ryan had taken a temporary job transfer to his company's Toronto office. It was more difficult to explain the sense of "calling" we had to this city, which, despite its warm welcome for immigrants (Toronto's population is nearly 50 percent immigrant), did not warmly embrace Christianity—or Christians. (A year later, my neighbor in Toronto, learning that I was "born-again," would nod with vague recognition, "I think I might know one other person like you.") Toronto is a city where the historic Christian faith is excluded from public discourse on the basis that it is backward and boorish. Toronto, characteristically polite, is politely hostile to orthodox faith: even the mention of attending church can be cause for dreaded awkwardness in friendly conversation.

Some of our friends felt concerned that we were moving to Toronto, not only because it was relentlessly secular but because, rather than homeschooling our children in Toronto as we had in Chicago, we would be enrolling them in school. One friend, another homeschooling mom, went so far as to ask, "What will it matter in heaven if your children speak French?"

First Things

Early in my Christian life, I understood belonging to Christ more—and belonging to his kingdom less. Salvation was often presented in my evangelical tradition as a faith transaction between a sinner and God. When the transaction was made, the sinner was guaranteed eternal life. *God loves you and has a wonderful plan for your life:* this was how I first came to understand the gospel. Salvation was primarily about getting to heaven, and the gospel was the means of getting you there (see Romans 1:16). As such, it served as a formula for a personal confession of faith. "Christ died for our sins, . . . was buried, . . . was raised on the third day in accordance with the Scriptures" (1 Corinthians 15:3-4).

The problem with this gospel of God's "wonderful plan for my life" (in addition to its inability to account for life's difficulties) was its constricted understanding of God's kingdom. The kingdom is a concept central not only to the Lord's Prayer but also to the entire gospel. An understanding of God's kingdom is even fundamental to answering our hesitations about desire, which are often rooted in our confusion over God's will. *What will it matter in heaven if your children speak French?* my friend had asked, and I can neither blame her nor dismiss her concern. However, I can regret that her question reveals the narrow categories by which many evangelicals have come to define the gospel, categories that don't allow for broader definitions of good. She revealed how handily so many Christians divorce heaven and earth, thinking that the gospel has only to do with the former and nothing with the latter. If we are to untangle our suspicions about desire, we have a desperate need for a more robust understanding of God's kingdom that will allow us the freedom to embrace our desires that don't, at first glance, feel "spiritual."

What will it matter in heaven if your kids speak French?

Kingdom is about God's first things. "Seek first the kingdom of God and his righteousness, and all these things will be added to you" (Matthew 6:33). This verse is an important one for any discussion of desire and finding God's will. When Jesus commands his followers to seek the kingdom, he is asking us to order our priorities. Put first things first. Pursue what really matters. *Kingdom* is a signpost toward the holy. It provides just the kind of steady hand we need for discerning our desires, pointing, as it does, in the direction of God's values and committing us to obedience. To pray "your kingdom come, your will be done," we express our desire (and God's!) that he rule over every corner of our lives, even over the entire creation. "There is not a square inch in the whole domain of our human existence over which Christ, who is Sovereign over all, does not cry: 'Mine!'" said Abraham Kuyper famously.[1] To pray the prayer for the kingdom coming, we face the inevitability that our desires must be subordinated to God's. Kingdom prayers grow in us the will to belong more fully to God.

> *Kingdom prayers grow in us the will to belong more fully to God.*

A cursory walk through the first four books of the New Testament has us tripping over the concept of kingdom, especially when we begin with the Gospel of Matthew: "The book of the genealogy of Jesus Christ, the son of David, the son of Abraham." Matthew begins by heralding this royal proclamation: Jesus Christ, son of Joseph and Mary, is heir to the throne of King David. He is the King for whom the world has long been waiting.

The reign and rule of Jesus Christ is the kingdom. And as we learn in the Lord's Prayer, God's people are to ask him to establish Jesus' reign and to accomplish his will. As they do, they can anticipate the culture of heaven descending to earth: *Your kingdom come, your will be done, on earth as it is in heaven.*

The Gospel writers record their eyewitness accounts of what the kingdom coming to earth really looks like. In the life and ministry of Jesus Christ, we see that our God has both spiritual and earthly preoccupations. Heaven mattered to Jesus, for sure, and proclaiming eternal salvation from sin was essential to Jesus' message of the kingdom. "As Moses lifted up the serpent in the wilderness, so must the Son of Man be lifted up, that whoever believes in him may have eternal life" (John 3:14-15). Jesus was insistent that sin was a very real problem, and because of sin, humans would be eternally separated from God apart from the divine work of atonement. But the stuff of earth mattered to Jesus too. In addition to his concern for the *souls* of men and women, Jesus also paid a good deal of attention to their *bodies*: hands that wouldn't work, backs that wouldn't straighten, legs that couldn't walk. The kingdom advanced as Jesus healed physical infirmities *and* proclaimed forgiveness from sin, took interest in the poor *and* the poor in spirit.

> The gospel of the kingdom announced this good news: God had a wonderful plan—for the world.

King Jesus was bringing redemption in all of its fullness, and the establishment of God's reign—his kingdom—inaugurated the campaign to heal all that was broken in the wake of human rebellion post-Genesis 3. The gospel of the kingdom announced this good news: God had a wonderful plan—for the world. Jesus' kingship recalibrated values—"blessed are the poor in spirit" (Matthew 5:3). It reorganized ambition—"do not lay up for yourselves treasures on earth" (Matthew 6:19). It also redefined loyalties—"follow me, and leave the dead to bury their own dead" (Matthew 8:22). "Jesus is

King" was no private confession of religious faith; its ambition was no less than remaking earth in the likeness of heaven. As twenty-first-century readers of a first-century Gospel, we may not immediately understand the bold, cataclysmic claim Matthew was making—and that Jesus made of himself when, launching into public ministry, he announced, "Repent, for the kingdom of heaven is at hand" (Matthew 4:17). To say that Jesus was King was to declare emphatically that Caesar was not. Jesus' claim to the throne was a declaration about his right to power. It insisted that the Roman emperor had been dethroned. And as it was a declaration of power, it was also a summons of allegiance. This new King Jesus deserved worship.

N. T. Wright, in his book *What Saint Paul Really Said,* situates the audacity of Jesus' claim to kingship for contemporary readers like this: "What would preachers of the gospel need to do today if people were to say of them what they said of Paul, that he was announcing, in the face of the claim of Caesar, that there was 'another king, namely Jesus'? They would need, for a start, to do what Paul did, namely, to confront the powers of the world with the news that their time is up, and that they owe allegiance to Jesus himself."[2] Wright acknowledges that Jesus' claim to kingship confronts our twenty-first-century gods as boldly and defiantly as it did the Roman Caesars.

If Jesus is king, our desires are turned upside down. We owe no more loyalty to the idols of status and popularity. If Jesus is king, we no longer bow at the feet of prestige and comfort. Money, sex and power—these are the gods dethroned when the kingdom of heaven is at hand. "When we are truly announcing the lordship of Jesus, we must make it clear that, according to this gospel, the one true God has dealt in Jesus Christ with sin, death, guilt and shame, and now summons men and women everywhere to abandon the idols which hold them captive to these things and to discover a new life, and a new way of life, in him."[3] "Jesus is King" is the pledge of allegiance to the one true God. The faith transaction, which I'd grown up believing was the moment I confessed my sin and claimed ownership of heaven, had far more profound implications for my life than simply determining where I would spend eternity after I died. I belonged to Christ—and his kingdom. This laid claim to my deepest desires, here and now.

Serve the Times

It's the *contemplatio* we're after. Like every other Sunday night, we've gathered for our weekly small group, having committed ourselves as a group to getting the text under our skin. We're studying Galatians 3, and the verse that hangs in the air that night is verse 8. "And the Scripture, foreseeing that God would justify the Gentiles by faith, preached the gospel beforehand to Abraham, saying, 'In you shall all the nations be blessed.'"

What many in the room can't seem to make sense of is the continuity between the Old and New Testaments to which the apostle Paul, in his letter to the Galatians, is referring. One man throws up his hands and admits his great difficulty in making any kind of connection between the Old and New Testaments. Others nod in agreement. Where are we to find the gospel in Genesis? Where is Jesus? Where is the cross, the resurrection? What did Abraham *admit, believe and confess*, and how can "blessed to be a blessing" be the gospel if it fails to explicitly mention sin, repentance, faith and salvation? Evangelical emphasis on personal faith (and the kingdom of God as equivalent to heaven) would seem to fail the exegesis of Genesis.

God has a wonderful plan for your life tells an important part of the gospel story, even if it fails to tell the whole. "If you confess with your mouth that Jesus is Lord and believe in your heart that God raised him from the dead, you will be saved," Paul says in Romans 10:9. Furthermore, at the opening of his letter to the Romans, Paul defends the gospel as "the power of God for salvation to everyone who believes" (Romans 1:16). In a real sense, the gospel is fundamentally concerned with spiritual salvation and the human response to God. The gospel reveals our desperate need, as men and women wrecked by sin, for divine forgiveness, which we have not deserved and could never earn. The gospel is the good news of Jesus' death on behalf of sinners, he taking the punishment we deserved and reversing the curse of death. "Death is swallowed up in victory. O death, where is your victory? O death, where is your sting?" (1 Corinthians 15:54-55). This message—of heaven— is *gospel.*

We've rightly fought battles for the doctrinal truths we consider so fundamental to the gospel. Dietrich Bonhoeffer died in a concentration camp in Nazi Germany for defending the gospel in his generation. "Only he who cries out for the Jews may sing Gregorian chants."[4] Bonhoeffer was part of the long historical parade of willing volunteers who resisted attempts to dilute and distort the historic truths of the Christian faith, even giving their life for the purity and protection of the gospel. Bonhoeffer believed in the need for every person to confess his faith in Jesus Christ for the forgiveness of his or her sins.

Nevertheless, Bonhoeffer never imagined that preaching the gospel equaled exclusive emphasis on a future eternal realm. He understood that the "first things" of the kingdom were often "earthly" commitments and concerns—the stuff of the here and now. "God wants to see human beings, not ghosts who shun the world. . . . If you want to find eternity, you must serve the times."[5] According to Bonhoeffer, the gospel of the kingdom doesn't put God's people on hold, leaving them with little to do but drum their fingers until the pearly gates of heaven open. The gospel is admission into heaven—but it is also mission. It implicates God's people in participation in activities of every kind that bless the world and bring the culture of heaven to earth.

In you shall all the nations be blessed.

❧

In *Circle of Quiet,* Madeleine L'Engle describes how her young adult novel *A Wrinkle in Time* was dismissed by eight publishers before it eventually landed with the publishing house of Farrar, Strauss and Giroux. For L'Engle, the decade of her thirties was set on the spin cycle of rejection. On her fortieth birthday, her husband called L'Engle in her writing studio to say that another rejection letter had come from yet another publisher. In a fit of melancholic despair, L'Engle shrouded her typewriter with a sheet. She would never write again.

Thankfully, her resolve did not last long. L'Engle asked for the manuscript back from her agent, and it arrived as a heavy parcel of bundled typewritten sheets. Two weeks later, with the manuscript in her possession, she was introduced to another editor. He asked to read the manuscript. In another week, she had signed a contract to publish *Wrinkle.*

> When the book was rejected by publisher after publisher, I cried out in my journal. I wrote, after an early rejection, "X turned down *Wrinkle,* turned it down with one hand while saying that he loved it, but didn't quite dare do it, as it isn't really classifiable. I know it isn't really classifiable . . . but this book I'm sure of. If I've ever written a book that says what I feel about God and the universe, this is it.
>
> This is my psalm of praise."[6]

❧

His father—my brother—committed suicide when he was only two. In the wake of that trauma, my nephew's mother worked at a daycare to keep him close to her. In those early years, the responsibilities of raising this blond-headed boy illuminated an inner incandescence in her that wouldn't be put out by financial worries or her troubled relationship with a live-in boyfriend. *Doing the best she can.* But our early years of optimism ceded to tumult. My nephew tells me now that he became a man at the age of six. It was then he learned the skill of calling the toll-free number on the back of his mother's EBT card. His childhood passed in the quiet anxiety between government checks. Some of his most vivid memories are hungry ones.

Jimmy visited our family after our first year in Toronto. At seventeen, he was talking college and even musing aloud about the family he might one day have. He was a boy with a wide circle of friends, scholastic accomplishment, even a well-developed emotional vocabulary despite the turbulence of those childhood years that were now behind him—and still, I noticed, palpably present in the sag of his shoulders. After his return to the States, I spent several days crying. My insides puddled up for reasons I couldn't explain.

As the weeks accumulated after Jimmy's return to West Virginia, I grew more and more certain that he should come to live with us after his high school graduation. My husband (who once told me I've never met an idea I didn't like) urged me to wait—and pray. And I could understand his hesitations. What sense did this make? Our nephew was almost eighteen. Presumably he'd be out on his own soon. We lived in Canada, had five children of our own! Where would he sleep? Attend university? And was it wise to bring him to Canada when we weren't even sure if we were staying in Toronto long term? There were forty-two and a half implausibilities.

The Gospel of Blessing

The gospel came two thousand years before Jesus Christ, to a veiled and sandaled shepherd in ancient Mesopotamia found driving his herds from Ur of the Chaldeans to the land of Canaan. Abram was told to leave the gods of his fathers and go. His faith and obedience were promised an eternal legacy of blessing. "In you shall all the nations be blessed," God told Abram (Galatians 3:8). "I will make of you a great nation, and I will bless you and make your name great, so that you will be a blessing" (Genesis 12:2). In this earliest representation of the gospel, we see it as God's pronouncement of blessing. God was blessing his people and making them a blessing. This circle of blessing would be completed in the redemptive events of the life of Abraham's ancestor, Jesus Christ: his death, burial and resurrection.

Abraham became the father of faith, and his faithfulness to God was measured by his capacity for taking God at his word. Long before the introduction of the law of Moses and its 613 commands, the Scriptures declare that Abraham was faithful and obedient: "Abraham obeyed my voice and kept my charge, my commandments, my statutes, and my laws" (Genesis 26:5). Abraham was congratulated for his faith. But he wasn't the first man of faith. Before Abraham, there was another man who walked with God and heeded the words of God. His name was Noah. He was commissioned to build a stadium-sized rescue boat when no cloud yet loomed in the sky. He and his family would witness the terrible judgment of God on earth, but when they emerged from the boat after the flood had subsided, like Abraham, they too were blessed: "Be fruitful and multiply and fill the earth" (Genesis 9:1). Noah, like Abraham, was blessed to be a blessing: here, too, is gospel.

But the gospel of God reaches further back—before Abraham, before Noah. The gospel comes to our human parents, Adam and Eve, the man and women whose created being crowned the creative work of God. They were made in the divine image. Before their plunge into sin and rebellion, they communed with God. "And God blessed them. And God said to them, 'Be fruitful and multiply and fill the earth and subdue it, and have dominion over the fish of the sea and over the birds of the heavens and over every living thing that moves on the earth" (Genesis 1:28). God settled the first man and woman in a lush and beautiful garden, providing for their abundant food, purposeful work, perfect relationships and his presence. He blessed them, asking that they, too, bless: this is gospel.

A clear pattern emerges in these first stories of the Bible: God blesses his people, freely and generously. His blessings indicate not human worthiness but divine benevolence. As if by reflex of character, God blesses. This is who he is; this is how he acts. He is eager to give good gifts to his people. This is the God of the gospel, a God whose liberality is love. The God of Genesis is the God we recognize in the New Testament, a God who so "*loved* the world that he gave his only Son,

> As if by reflex of character, God blesses.

that whoever believes in him should not perish but have eternal life" (John 3:16). Genesis anticipates the telling of this good news.

The blessing of God's people is meant for at least two reasons: first, to bind his people into loving communion with him. Adam and Eve, Noah, and Abraham—they walked with God. They enjoyed his presence. This was their greatest blessing. But it also obligated them to bless others beyond themselves. With Adam and Eve, God commissioned their stewardship on the basis of his blessing: I give you the land. Now rule it well. He gave every tree of the garden for their nourishment, excepting only one: "But of the tree of the knowledge of good and evil you shall not eat, for in the day that you eat of it you shall surely die" (Genesis 2:17). After the flood, God renewed the call of land and animal stewardship. He commended to Noah and his family a plentiful omnivore diet— "Every moving thing that lives shall be food for you. And as I gave you the green plants, I give you everything"—but he admonished, "you shall not eat flesh with its life, that is, its blood" (Genesis 9:3-4). Generations later, God initiated a generous promise of land and family, but those blessings invited Abraham's responsiveness to the divine imperative: "Go from your country and your kindred and your father's house to the land that I will show you" (Genesis 12:1). God blesses. We obey. We don't obey in order to be blessed, and we aren't blessed because our obedience has met divine performance standards. But blessing and obedience do comfortably and mysteriously coexist.

In the garden—in the kingdom—God's people are meant to look to him as the loving, predictable source of all good things. This inspires our *obedience* to him as well as our *desire* to be a blessing. Returning to these first stories in Genesis releases us into new freedoms of desire: first, to want good from God; second, to want to bless. God is a giver, and his desire is to bless his people. He is always driven toward generosity. We are right to desire benefit from him, and in asking for this good, we affirm our faith in his character. But the blessings we receive from God are never meant to be terminal: we recycle them. We obediently participate in big and small ways to bring heaven to earth.

> God is a giver, and his desire is to bless his people.

This theological groundwork helps us reach a holy equilibrium in desire. We can rid ourselves of the haunting fears that desiring good from God is selfish—it is, in fact, a primal response to his characteristic goodness. But in wanting good, we also commit to channeling good—to bless others as liberally and as sacrificially as we have been blessed. After all, in Christ, we are Abraham's children to whom the good-news promise is given: *In you shall all the nations be blessed.*

Babylon

As the Lord's Prayer would teach us, to be committed to the kingdom of God is to be committed to the honor of God's name. Genesis 11, sandwiched between two genealogies, tells a predictable story of human rebellion. The literary structure of the Tower of Babel narrative is deliberate. The tragic story is prefaced by the family line of Eber, as it issues from his son, Joktan. Joktan's story ends badly, in Babylon, or Babel (Genesis 11:1-9). In some sense, Joktan and his family live the story of those who willfully reject

God's rule and the honor of God's name. In defiance of God's commands, even God's blessings, they make self-aggrandizing plans. "Come, let us build ourselves a city and a tower with its top in the heavens, and let us make a name for ourselves, lest we be dispersed over the face of the whole earth" (Genesis 11:4). The name of greatest importance is not God's but their own. The project of greatest importance is self-designed. They don't want a kingdom; they want self-rule.

Genesis 11 opens with a migration: "As people moved eastward, they found a plain in Shinar and settled there" (v. 2 NIV). Moments of eastern migration have special significance in the Bible:

- "He drove out the man, and at the east of the garden of Eden he placed the cherubim and a flaming sword that turned every way to guard the way to the tree of life" (Genesis 3:24).

- "Then Cain went away from the presence of the LORD and settled in the land of Nod, east of Eden" (Genesis 4:16).

- "So Lot chose for himself all the Jordan Valley, and Lot journeyed east" (Genesis 13:11).

To the original readers, this indication in Genesis 11 that the people were heading east would have inspired dread. "In the Genesis narratives, when people go 'east,' they leave the land of blessing (Eden and the Promised Land) and go to a land where their greatest hopes will turn to ruin (Babylon and Sodom)," writes one commentator on this passage.[7] The people in Genesis 11 travel east, away from the direction of God's blessing and in deliberate opposition to God's command to "fill the earth and subdue it." They reject the good gift of land and choose as a substitute the domestication of a city. They reinterpret good and define for themselves what is best. The price of the project is the exchange of glory: human glory for God's. *Let us make a name for ourselves.*

Again, John Sailhamer, author of *The Pentateuch as Narrative*, writes:

The focus of the author since the beginning chapters of Genesis has been both on God's plan to bless humankind by providing them with that which is "good" and on the human failure to trust God and enjoy the "good" that God has provided. The characteristic mark of human failure up to this point in the book has been the attempt to grasp the "good" on their own rather than to trust God to provide it for them.[8]

Sailhamer provides an extraordinary summation of the nature of sin as we see it in the first third of Genesis. Humans want life on their own terms.

Rachel Marie Stone frames this same problem in her book, *Eat with Joy*:

> God *wants* to feed his people. In keeping the one tree from them, God protected Adam and Eve. When they broke table fellowship with God, they suspected that God was withholding something good, that this "good" would make them *like God*. . . . Just like in Eden, it's hard to trust that God isn't going to hold back the good things, the *best* things: that reaching out and taking what God is offering is really the best.[9]

And here is how desire becomes corrupt: wanting derails into selfishness, greed and demanding ingratitude when we've failed to recognize and receive the good that God has already given. Trust is at the center of holy desire: trust that God is good and wills good for his people. We trust in asking; we trust in receiving. Holy trust believes that whatever God chooses to give is enough.

> *Holy trust believes that whatever God chooses to give is enough.*

The Tower of Babel, the construction site of human pride, later becomes the city of Babylon in the biblical narrative. Babylon, in the Old and even the New Testament (in the book of Revelation), is the anti-kingdom. It is the place—real and figurative—where God is not worshiped. Hundreds of years later, the nation of Israel is eventually exiled to Babylon from the land God had promised to Abraham and given to his descendants. The exile proves the suicidal end of self-sovereignty. When we refuse God's good, when we mistrust God's intentions, when we clamor for self-rule, we exact the cruel price of suffering.

> By the waters of Babylon,
>> there we sat down and wept,
>> when we remembered Zion.
> On the willows there
>> we hung up our lyres.
> For there our captors
>> required of us songs,
> And our tormentors, mirth, saying,
>> "Sing us one of the songs of Zion!"
> How shall we sing the LORD's song
>> in a foreign land? (Psalm 137:1-4)

This is Joktan's disastrous story, which precedes the story of the Tower of Babel. It is Israel's story of rebellion. It is often our story too—on every occasion that we journey east. However, Joktan's story isn't the only story Genesis tells. There is another list of names—the family of Eber, and the son, Peleg. And Peleg's story ends more hopefully—with the three sons of Terah. One son is named Abraham. And Abraham is, of course, the father of faith, the one to whom the Pentateuch points as an example worthy of imitation. If Joktan's story is the narrative of self-sovereignty (and anti-kingdom), Peleg's story (and Abraham's) is the story of faithfulness and obedience. Through Jesus Christ, it can become our story too.

We can read Genesis 11 as a metaphor for human desire: we aren't easily satisfied by what God gives. We don't easily surrender to God's authority, and we are hell-bent on making a name for ourselves. Sinful desire has a cruel way of leading us out of God's kingdom to Babylon, where we impertinently define good and then demand that

God provide it on our terms. Those desires are neither trusting nor
surrendered, and they lead us into the land of exile. And though it
would seem that the forces of evil desire are strong, the Lord's Prayer
is one force of resistance: these words are arms we bear, this prayer
is ground we stand when the lure of east feels almost irresistible:

> Our Father in heaven,
> hallowed be your name.
> Your kingdom come,
> Your will be done.
> on earth as it is in heaven.

These words form in us a desire for kingdom, a longing for the first
things, even that God's name be honored above our own. It's not an
incantation by which we are mesmerized and led unthinking into
a life of mechanical obedience. It is immersive language into which
we plunge to begin imagining what a life surrendered to King Jesus
really resembles. They are words we pray, not always because we
believe them but because we want to believe them.

If Genesis 11 is our story, we can be consoled by the graciousness
of God on display in Babel. At the end of the narrative of the Tower
of Babel, the good news of rescue is close at hand. The final act of
God, in response to the rebellion of Babel, is an act not of judgment
but of grace. "The LORD dispersed them from there over the face of
all the earth, and they left off building the city" (Genesis 11:8).
Initially, I had read this to mean that God flung them to the four
corners of the earth in the fury of his judgment. But Sailhamer interprets this verse differently: "God moved to rescue them from
those plans [to build Babylon] and return them to the land and the
blessing that awaited them there."[10] God's movement toward his
wandering people was gracious, not punitive.

Sinfully, we seem to want to reject kingdom, preferring to God's
throne our towers of self-importance. But because of the kingdom
of God, which comes to rule in our hearts through grace by faith,

God graciously rescues us from ourselves and sets us back in the path of blessing. It is not self-effort that orients us toward the values and priorities of God's kingdom. It is not determination of will that positions us to receive his blessings: *sola gratia.* Grace—it means simply this: God, by his own efforts and unflagging energy, recalibrates our heart's desire for his kingdom. He leads us back to blessing, even when, traveling the road of desire, we would journey east.

Your kingdom come, your will be done, on earth as it is in heaven.

> God, by his own efforts and unflagging energy, recalibrates our heart's desire for his kingdom.

Remake God's World

The gospel in Genesis—and the self-sacrificing love of Jesus—insists that our lives should be shaped by the desire to bless. The word *blessing* is such a simple one—and I often need simple words to wade through the inordinate complications I make of my life, especially my faith. As a word, blessing reconciles ways and means. It is a relational word, a word that incarnates me in my place and commissions me to mend my small corner of the world with acts of kindness and love. *Blessing* is the word that brings our family to Toronto. It brings my nephew into our family. It even births a book. *Blessing* is a word of counter-formation: though the world will insist that the good life can be measured by what is achieved and accumulated, Jesus reminds me that my good is found in another's—in my acts of giving and giving away.

To bless the world in the name of Jesus Christ is to participate in the both/and activity of the gospel. As Christ-followers, we are called to clearly proclaim that sin is the fundamental human problem—and that Jesus Christ dealt with human sin on the cross, reconciling people to God through faith and reversing the curse of death.

> Knowing the fear of the Lord, we persuade others. . . . For the love of Christ controls us, because we have concluded this: that one has died for all, therefore all have died; and he

died for all, that those who live might no longer live for themselves, but for him who for their sake died and was raised. (2 Corinthians 5:11, 14-15)

The desire to tell others the *euangelion* of Jesus Christ is necessary for kingdom participation—and I admit that I don't come to this desire as easily as I want. Praying "Your kingdom come, your will be done" should generate in each of us the desire for the salvation of those we love who do not yet know and trust Christ. It should compel us to turn conversations with these friends and family, as often as seems natural, in the direction of spiritual truth. The greatest blessing any of us shares is friendship with God, and we should want to be faithful to offer that gift to others.

To be committed to clear gospel proclamation is right, and it is also right to bless the world in ways more intangibly connected to the gospel of Christ's kingdom. *What will it matter if your children speak French?* my friend had asked when we were considering a move to Toronto. On the surface there would seem to be no eternal value to learning a second language, but we cannot underestimate what God will do with any and all of our skills, gifts, interests and desires that we surrender fully to him. The ability to speak another language, to write a novel, to repair a car, to lead a business, to welcome an orphan—these, too, can be offered to King Jesus and to the remaking of his world. Each can serve as acts of blessing.

Ins Choi, a Christian playwright in Toronto, once told me how his play *Kim's Convenience* blessed the city of Toronto without having been explicitly evangelistic. "It makes people laugh, makes them cry, and makes them see something in themselves that they were blind to." Blessing one's city through art is not like other vocational callings, Choi insisted. "It's like teaching, plumbing and building good furniture. [We should] make lamps that work, that are aesthetically pleasing, and that serve the common good." The play was an enormous success in Toronto, especially as it spoke into the tensions of the immigrant experience. "When people left the theatre," Dan MacDonald, Choi's pastor (and mine), said, "they left thinking through their own family, spirituality, and connection to the city. Very few people can say eighty minutes of their lives did that."[11]

In you all the families of the earth shall be blessed.

Each of us has a role to play in the advancement of Christ's kingdom. To be formed into Christ is to fully desire—and fully commit—to the coming of God's kingdom. To pray Jesus' prayer "Your kingdom come, your will be done" is to be drafted into the call of God. This may obligate us to preach, to write, to move or to speak French. It will certainly ask us to reach out to tangibly love

> To be formed into Christ is to fully desire—and fully commit—to the coming of God's kingdom.

those in our closest circles of influence. But the best news of all is that the establishment of God's kingdom will never fully depend on us—thank God. "The kingdom of God is as if a man should scatter seed on the ground. He sleeps and rises night and day, and the seed sprouts and grows; he knows not how. The earth produces by itself, first the blade, then the ear, then the full grain in the ear. But when the grain is ripe, at once he puts in the sickle, because the harvest has come" (Mark 4:26-29). The kingdom is established by God's work, not ours. And this, too, is grace into which we lean.

Reflection Questions

1. If trust is at the center of holy desire, what makes it easy or difficult for you to trust God?

2. How do you personally experience the lure of *east*?

3. Consider how the word *blessing* adds congruence to the diversity of your kingdom callings. What desires does this word release in you?

5

Visions of Sugarplums

Scripture

There's no use crying over spilled milk—unless, of course, you live at my house. Spilled milk is part of our regular dinnertime festivities. So, too, is the crying. At dinnertime, we gather as peaceably as a coop full of clucking, hungry chickens. I'd like to think of the time we spend around the table as inviolable, sacred even, but our elbows always prove unsanctimonious. Milk spills.

And pools—inevitably meandering toward the crevice between the table leaves. Then seeps—slowly to the floor. And someone will come to regret their act of carelessness when they mop up the milk with a clutch of paper towels, carry the soppy mess back to the sink and feel my disapproval burn at their back. Spilled milk has potential for becoming a household disaster.

Dinnertime is no adagio ending to the day. It keeps to an irregular beat, plays loud and arrhythmic with interruption. Dinner is a cacophonous exercise of holy sanctification long before the dishes have ever been cleared and Ryan has opened the Scriptures and attempted to lead the hen house in prayer. But when he does finally take the leather-bound book into his hands, it signals for quiet. We the chickens settle into a version of mock docility.

Sometimes, it even passes for reverence.

I was sixteen when I began reading the Bible regularly. Having been strangely plucked from prodigal existence at summer camp, I was sent back, after a week, into a world that was no longer familiar to me. I was even unfamiliar to myself. I knew that life had been irrevocably altered, and this was no more apparent than on the evening of my return from camp, when my boyfriend and I sat stiffly across from one another on the couch in my family room.

"I don't want to sleep with you anymore."

All those growing up years in the church, and I didn't know what it felt like to grow up with faith. I didn't know how faith felt when it grew incrementally, developing steadily as if climbing the plot line of a growth chart, stretching upward and outward with stature and the natural lengthening of limbs. I only knew conversion like mine, which, at its origin, felt like a cataclysmic dislocation. Learning to live with faith after prodigal-hood was like beginning, after a stroke, the long and deliberate process of rehabilitation. If I ever knew how to walk, now I needed to learn again. If I ever knew how to speak, now I needed to learn again. All the skills I had once mastered had to be relearned. My first task was standing upright. *Now one foot, now the other.*[1]

The counselors at the summer camp I had attended at the age of sixteen warned the newly converted among us against flash-in-the-pan faith, and they challenged us to take up regular spiritual practices for the next six months. Pray for five minutes a day. Read the Bible for ten minutes a day. Tell another person about Jesus every week. (As it was a Southern Baptist camp, I seem also to remember that we foreswore alcohol for the rest of our lives.) These were the habits of faithfulness we were to put on—and hope to wear for a lifetime.

I'm sure these commitments sound legalistic. I'm also sure I kept them in that spirit for years. And though daily spiritual disciplines could reduce the desire for God into dry, perfunctory routine (think math facts), in my own life they inaugurated a beautiful, nearly invisible process of rehabilitation. I am different—and want differently—for the now thousands of days I've begun in the Bible.

Holy Playbook of Desire

Scripture is the bedrock in the life of a Christian, and it is hard—impossible almost—to grow without it, especially if one wants to grow a life of holy desire. People do, of course, and historically they have. (After all, it's only been five centuries since the Bible was first translated into the language of the common people.) But I don't recommend neglect if we can help it.

The Bible reads like a theological playbook of desire. Psalm 119, for example, is an acrostic poem celebrating the holy perfection of Scripture and the blessedness of obedience to God's laws. It provocatively evokes desire.

> "Open my eyes, that I may behold *wondrous* things out of your law" (v. 18).

> "My soul is consumed with *longing* for your rules at all times" (v. 20).

> "Your testimonies are my *delight*; they are my counselors" (v. 24).

> "The law of your mouth is *better* to me than thousands of gold and silver pieces" (v. 72).

> "Consider how I *love* your precepts! Give me life according to your steadfast love" (v. 159).

The entire psalm reads like a prayer of desire: *Father, teach me to want rightly, and help me to live in obedience to those right desires.* Psalm 119 exalts the truth, wisdom and goodness of God's word and commends the practice of reading the Scriptures for growing into a life of obedience. But the obedience to which it calls God's people is obedience inspired by the marvel of God and the beauty of his commands. It is obedience predicated on renovated, rehabilitated and renewed desire—desire that is turned toward God. As we internalize this kind of desire by reading the Scriptures, obedience eventually becomes organic and reflexive. *Now one foot, now the other.*

The Bible plots our course of counterformation. We read it—and imbibe the values of Christ and his kingdom. We read it—and submit ourselves to the process of being shaped into the people of God who want differently than the world wants.

> Do not love the world or the things in the world. If anyone loves the world, the love of the Father is not in him. For all that is in the world—the desires of the flesh and the desires of the eyes and pride of life—is not from the Father but is from the world. And the world is passing away along with its desires, but whoever does the will of God abides forever. (1 John 2:15-17)

Our allegiance to the Father is strengthened as we learn to identify the difference between godly desires and worldly desires. The Bible serves as a field guide for exactly that kind of project.

The Lord's Prayer is, of course, one small portion of Scripture that has interested me in my exploration of holy desire. Opening with the address *Our Father*, the prayer begs important questions: Who is God? What does he want for me? These questions stand central in the pursuit of Christian desire, and the only reliable means we have for answering them is by examining the Scriptures. Desire, if it's to be trusted, should be inspired by a divine vocabulary.

The Lord's Prayer teaches us to value what is supremely valuable—*Father, kingdom.* It also teaches us to want for a better world—*on earth as it is in heaven.* It even pro-

> *Desire, if it's to be trusted, should be inspired by a divine vocabulary.*

vides the lens for seeing why we are so often dissatisfied with life in the everyday. "We learn [from the Bible] that through all of life there runs a ground note of cosmic disappointment," writes Tim

Keller in *Counterfeit Gods,* "that no matter what we put our hopes in . . . it is always Leah and never Rachel."[2] C. S. Lewis also spoke to this current of disappointment running through the human experience: "Most people, if they have really learned to look into their own hearts, would know that they do want, and want acutely, something that cannot be had in this world. There are all sorts of things in this world that offer to give it to you, but they never quite keep their promise."[3] The world is a disappointing place. As St. Augustine said, we are restless until our hearts find their rest in God.

This must be why our desires are met with frequent disappointment. My friend Wendy calls the incremental disappointments we endure over the years "the slow leak of life." And if the ordinarily beautiful experiences of babies and seaside vacations, career and lifelong love, as Lewis later describes, cease to ultimately satisfy the profound longings of the human soul, and if, as Keller says, the "ground note" of life is a melancholy one, imagine what faces us in the moments of our greatest loss. It is not easy to want in a life like this one. This is why loss is an important story to tell if we mean to be faithful in any discussion of desire—and why the Scriptures are an important hand to hold.

Our Father.

The Sideways Life

Possibilities can do their dying—before marriage and children, bills and grey hair. Possibilities can do their dying in your eighteenth year, betraying you and your optimism the moment your father falls dead, dressed in his overcoat with a briefcase beside him. On that day, a stranger finds you in a crowded dining hall. She asks your name, tells you to follow her, and just beyond the din of the college cafeteria, directs you to the pay phone. *Call home.* You will remember each of these details vividly, only vaguely remembering what happens once you reach your mother on the other end and she tells you your father is dead and you need to fly home.

There is, as you picture it, the sight of you collapsing against the wall and sliding to the floor.

Possibilities do their dying—in airports, as you watch the world in your haunting new way, observing the people strolling past and wondering how they, too, have been saddened by surprise endings, made grim by their real-life possibilities. You will learn to wonder who is catching a plane to meet her mother and whose father will fail to make the appearance she expects.

As I discovered in March of my freshmen year of college, life has the inauspicious capability of driving like a reckless drunk. It careens off course, leaving no time to respond or react, no moment of clarity and courage for bracing against the impact. My father was dead. I was eighteen. And only two days earlier, he had celebrated his forty-ninth birthday. By all appearances, he was a healthy man.

Life changes fast.
Life changes in an instant.
You sit down for dinner, and life as you know it ends.
The question of self-pity.[4]

In her book *The Year of Magical Thinking*, Joan Didion chronicles her shock and disorienting grief after her own sideways event. On a December evening, Didion and her husband had sat down for dinner in their Manhattan apartment. Her husband collapsed mid-sentence, a fork raised to his mouth, a sentence strangled in his throat. Arriving after her 911 call, the paramedics pumped her husband's chest and injected his body with epinephrine in the middle of their living room, but despite all their desperate efforts, he did not revive.

You sit down for dinner, and life as you know it ends.

Didion's book tolls the refrain of the sideways life. Neglecting the rules of courtesy, the sideways life screeches to an unwelcome stop on the most ordinary of days: around a table at dinnertime; in spring, when the daffodils and crocuses have only just burst into bloom. Sideways scenes arrive with such gale force precisely because we do not ever see them coming.

"Time is a relentless river. It rages on, a respecter of no one," writes Ann Voskamp.[5] In the first chapter of her best-selling book, *One Thousand Gifts,* Voskamp describes how, standing "in November light, I see my mother and father sitting on the back porch step rocking her swaddled body in their arms. . . . Blood seeps through the blanket bound."[6] Her little sister had toddled into the farm lane and been killed by a delivery driver.

Each of us is moved in the unpredictable currents of today, and existence can feel as weightless as an amputated branch dislodged in a storm. We spin, catch, break free, drown and surface, all the while driven by the fickleness of time's wind and weather. Whatever awaits us tomorrow, it is quite possibly not a scene we have expected, nor an act for which we have prepared.

Where is God when life goes sideways—when *you sit down to dinner and life as you know it ends*? Has God, as we have sometimes imagined him, stood idly by, preoccupied with the more pressing affairs of the universe? How do we say that God is good when life is not? And what, if anything, can be made of the prayers we've whispered in the middle of nights, restless with fear and the threat of loss, prayers that have had no apparent answer, no just-in-the-nick-of-time rescue?

Who can be made to want in a world so cruel? These doubts drive a deep canyon of despair through the landscape of desire.

❧

He was strong and muscular. *Fifteen.* As a group, they'd shrugged off their mothers' last hugs and left Chicago for the Upper Peninsula of Michigan, where they'd planned, along with several other church groups, to spend a week completing much-needed construction projects. Five boys, their pastor, benevolence and the will of God packed for good measure. When Thursday's sun dawned, they gave themselves over to a day of rest and recreation, entering the placid surf of Lake Superior. Their laughter, indifferent to wind and weather, rose with the waves.

Tempestuous, temperamental Lake Superior. Even though she was known to act on caprice, no one had expected her mood to shift. And no one would anticipate the horror when three of the boys were pulled under that day, held in the lethal grip of a rip tide.

Her son drowned that day.

My friend tells me how cold his body felt on the day they had gone to identify the lifeless form pulled from a cabinet of cadavers. She laid her head on the nakedness. It had been her habit to wake him this way: her head to his chest, she maternally synchronized to the predictable rhythms of his morning breathing.

At the morgue that day, there had been only the whir of refrigeration.

❧

Contingency is language I borrow from Stanley Hauerwas's memoir, *Hannah's Child*. In the book, Hauerwas describes not only his work as a theologian but the nearly twenty-five years he had stayed married to a woman with mental illness. Every day that Hauerwas was married to Anne was an unpredictable one. Neither he nor his son, Adam, could ever say with confidence which wife and mother they'd find at the end of each day, given as she was to abandoning reality without formal announcement. "To say that our lives are contingent is to say that they are out of our control."[7]

This prospect of out-of-control living unhinges us. We prefer the not wanting and the not having to the losing. Like a spigot gushing uncertainty, we turn off desire to prevent it leaking hope. We anesthetize desire, we numb the heart—and this can feel like the safest choice in lives destined for collision with loss. How can we be made to want in this world

> Until Jesus returns and puts all of his enemies under his feet, every human relationship will resolve into loss.

"where all human relationships end in pain, [this being] the price that our imperfection has allowed Satan to exact from us for the privilege of love?"[8] To dust we are destined to return. Rage as we might against mortality's belligerence, the bald fact is that until Jesus returns and puts all of his enemies under his feet, every human relationship will resolve into loss (see 1 Corinthians 15:25-26).

§

She had wanted a baby. The desire for a child had throbbed silently through the years of her greying. But she does not admit this desire to the prophet Elisha, who regularly passes through her village and dines with her and her husband.

She not only regularly invites Elisha to stay for supper, but she's drawn up plans for a house renovation so that Elisha can have his own bedroom. She hangs the windows with curtains, lights a lamp at his desk and smoothes the sheets on his bed. This little room becomes a personal bed and breakfast for the prophet of God.

"What is to be done for her?" Elisha asks his servant Gehazi, overcome with the generosity of this wealthy matron of Shunem (2 Kings 4:13).

"Well, she has no son, and her husband is old," Gehazi answers.

"Call her."

She arrives, but the text pictures the Shunammite woman as if she is reluctant to enter the room. She lingers in the doorway, rooted as if in some kind of weathered hesitation. She is affixed, transfixed, planted. She wears doubt heavy.

"At this season, about this time next year," Elisha announces to her, "you shall embrace a son" (v. 16).

"No, my lord, O man of God; do not lie to your servant." The Shunammite cannot hope so extravagantly, and this good news is unwelcome. When a woman has lived so long abandoning the impossibilities of desire, it is not easy to pick it up again.

Nevertheless, the prophecy is fulfilled. She and her husband welcome a son into their arms. The text is silent on the years of his growing up, but with faith we imagine them to be years that prosper their love.

You sit down to dinner and life as you know it ends.

"When the child had grown, he went out one day to his father among the reapers. And he said to his father, 'Oh my head, my head!' The father said to his servant, 'Carry him to his mother.' And when he had lifted him and brought him to his mother, the child sat on her lap till noon, and then he died" (2 Kings 4:18-20).

Why, I can't help but ask, does God conceive promise only to give birth to death?

$$\clubsuit$$

I live another sideways scene.

This time, I am twenty-three. My husband and I have celebrated our first wedding anniversary and leave Chicago dressed in a flaming palate of fall. We travel to Ohio for the wedding of friends. Two days later, on our way home, we stop to visit with my great-aunt, and around her kitchen table, we laugh and nurse cups of the blond, sweet coffee she taught me to drink when I was still a girl in pigtails. The telephone rings. It is my mother. My brother is dead; she has found him in the garage behind the wheel of her car. All the years of addiction and depression, the ledger of accumulated regrets and unbearable sadness—he has ended them, erased it without warning, without explanation, and we are left with the unanswerable and silent shame that suicide visits upon a family.

You sit down to dinner, and life as you know it ends.

The Test of Revelation

Our Father.

We do not hold these truths to be self-evident: God is good, and he loves us. God's goodness cannot always be empirically verified by our life experience, and we are cast not upon skills of deduction but upon the muddled exercise called faith. Faith—should we want it to be real and substantial, based on the objective truth of who God is and how he is at work in the world—"comes from hearing, and hearing through the word of Christ" (Romans 10:17). Faith, if it is to be called such, must be inspired by the language of the Scriptures, even if the assertions and conclusions we find there surprise us.

As a culture, we seem to be smugly sure of our capacities for reason. We don't readily submit to the idea that we must be taught. But as a people of faith, faith in the one true God who has revealed himself through Christ and the Word, we know there is truth, which is spiritually revealed and spiritually discerned (1 Corinthians 2:6-14). "The natural person does not accept the things of the Spirit of God, for they are folly to him, and he is not able to understand them" (v. 14). If faith is dependent on illumination by the sacred texts of Scripture, so, too, is desire.

Most of us have had the experience of wanting and waiting, of praying and not receiving the answers for which we've prayed. Were we to be honest, every occasion of disappointment, every loss seems to call into question the goodness of God. We wonder why he doesn't do more to protect us from the life driving recklessly out of control. Why doesn't he heed our wanting and hoping, our praying and believing? How can our Father be good in the midst of such devastating loss?

> Every occasion of disappointment, every loss seems to call into question the goodness of God.

When Joan Didion began writing for *Life* magazine, one reader wrote to the editor to complain that "your new writer, Joan Didion, is not exactly, 'Little Mary Sunshine,' is she?"[9] I may be similarly accused. Having shared these dramatic stories of loss, I've transported us, as it were, to the valley of the shadow of death. And though it will seem strange to include stories of loss in a book about desire, like a doctor who amputates a limb in order to save a life, I want to do away with our gangrened expectations about what life, even God, owes us.

Who is God? The Bible teaches that God is inexorably good. "You are good and do good" (Psalm 119:68). Because God is good, he wills good for his people. This doctrine injects courage into the act of desire: God wants what is best, for me and for the world. Nevertheless, God's goodness—for he *is* good and *does* good—is no saccharine version of *Your Best Life Now.* To say that God is good is not the same thing as saying that life is good. To say that God is faithful is not to say that he will spare us the searing realities of pain and loss. To say that God sovereignly supervises the world is not to deny that life appears, at least from our vantage point, to be advancing according to principles of indifference, even malfeasance.

Perhaps this is why faith seems like such a ridiculous enterprise to the world at large. Why cling so desperately to the improbable notion of divine providence? Why affirm that the world is anything but a heartless place? Why keep at incredulity, why assert the impossibility of hope?

> To say that God is good is not the same thing as saying that life is good.

Why want?

A friend asks me exactly this. I am curled up on a corner of her couch, a cup of tea warming my hands on this blustery April day, which resembles winter more than spring. Faith has frozen over for her and her husband in the past year. They'd come to Toronto so that he could complete a master's program and had hoped this would position him to apply for PhD programs. After they had moved internationally and she had suffered through a couple of years of mindless work (limited by a provisional visa from doing anything more meaningful), they spent their meager savings on his graduate school applications. They prayed. They believed. They heaved mustard seeds at their mountains. But eleven applications met with rejection. The only favorable reply had included an impossibly small stipend on which they could not hope to live. If these rejections weren't enough, as they straddled their uncertainty of what next, hanging suspended over the chasm of growing doubts about God's nearness, she miscarried. Hope too.

I don't want to offer anyone tidy answers for what remains inexplicably messy and complex. Doubt won't be driven away by explanation. But I do believe there is a way to weather the temperamental wind and waves of our sideways events. We can hold fast. Or rather, *be held* fast. We don't have to deny the senseless horrors of life in order to defend God's goodness. We don't have to understand the mechanics of the universe. But even in the midst of doubt, we can keep tethering ourselves to what is true—though we cannot see it or believe it to be so. We can read the Scriptures, nudging our hearts toward the direction of believing this: God is good, and he loves us. This is the eternal work of faith as the Bible builds it, brick by theological brick.

And perhaps the most important reason why faith will flounder apart from the Scriptures is because the Bible testifies to the central event of saving faith: the cross of Jesus Christ. A crucified Savior? At the cross, in the horror of death and the agony of ultimate loss, God meets us in our moments of greatest incredulity and doubt. The cross of Jesus Christ assures us of this wildly improbable proposition that God can remain good in the face of disfiguring loss, even death, and the cross defends the truth that "sometimes God seems to be killing us when he's actually saving us."[10] We may not have what we immediately want—and this may be God's best for us.

God is good, ultimately good. But he is also a God of mystery and surprise, a God whose ways cannot be patterned or predicted. He is not a God to be paid with quarters of prayer, dispensing candied, sweet goodness at our insistence. The sideways life and its deep wounds we call betrayals surface the true object of our faith. Do we want a master, or shall we have a genie whose command is our wish? This is the tension of desire—and the test of revelation.

I Am

We are each prone to the reshaping and reforming of God into our image. When we do this, we bow to the work of our own hands. This is especially dangerous to the proposition of desire. We can easily make a god who is preferential to requests, immediately responsive to our needs and committed to the achievement of our plans. This god will never ask us to relinquish our desires; he's as intent upon our self-sovereignty as we are. He will never visit upon us the undesirable; he's too nice for that.

But to confuse this god with Yahweh is a dangerous notion, as dangerous now as it was for the wandering Hebrews who pined for Egypt and, upon Moses' long absence, demanded

> *We can easily make a god who is preferential to requests, immediately responsive to our needs and committed to the achievement of our plans.*

of his brother, Aaron, "'Up, make us gods who shall go before us!'" (Exodus 32:1). Handed a graving tool and an assorted collection of jewelry, Aaron was all too quick to comply. "These are your gods, O Israel, who brought you up out of the land of Egypt!" (Exodus 32:4).

We, like the Israelites, have a hankering for idolatry, an appetite for gods of our own design. The fallen human project is this endless revising of God, and our only rescue from this chronic editorial impulse is to affirm the doctrine of revelation and to pledge allegiance to God as he has revealed himself to be. He is good, though not in all the ways that we expect him to be.

"'If I come to the people of Israel and say to them, "The God of your fathers has sent me to you," and they ask me, "What is his name?" what shall I say to them?' God said to Moses, 'I AM WHO I AM'" (Exodus 3:13-14). The I Am God announced to Israel that he would be worshiped on the terms he would declare. "You shall have no other gods before me. You shall not make for yourself a carved image, or any likeness of anything that is in heaven above, or that is in the earth beneath, or that is in the water under the earth" (Exodus 20:3-4). He is the *I Am who I Am*, not the *I Am who they wish.*

The God of Israel prohibited anyone from making a carved image in his likeness, a command that his people quickly forgot and transgressed. His "featurelessness," as G. K. Chesterton has called it, was intended to preserve the truth of his identity. The refusal to give God a face and a body was to allow for the infinite space, which God, in the truth of his being, occupies. The prohibition of carved images prevented the holy dimensions of his character from being constricted by human imagination.

"No eye has seen, nor ear heard, nor the heart of man imagined, what God has prepared for those who love him" (1 Corinthians 2:9). Faith is the capacity for believing that the God of the Scriptures is more real and more true than the gods of my own imaginative design. The God who is revealed in the Bible is better than good—even when I struggle to believe him to be so. And the God of the Scriptures is infinitely wise—even when I struggle to understand his purposes and imperatives. He is this because the Bible insists on it.

Jesus loves me, this I know, for the Bible tells me so.

The Bedside of Miracle

The Shunammite woman lays the body of her dead son on the prophet's bed. Closing the door behind her, she is deliberately evasive with her husband.

"Send me one of the servants and one of the donkeys, that I may quickly go to the man of God and come back again" (2 Kings 4:22).

Astride her donkey, impatiently bidding the animal to hurry, the woman approaches the mountain where the man of God, Elisha, makes his home. He sees her coming, and something about her stride speaks crisis. He tells Gehazi to run and to meet her, to ask, "Is all well with you? Is all well with your husband? Is all well with the child?" (v. 26).

But the woman won't suffer Gehazi and his questions. Instead, she advances, finally falling in a fit of sobs at the feet of Elisha. "Did I ask my lord for a son? Did I not say, 'Do not deceive me?'" (v. 28). Her mother hearts breaks open, bleeds for the extinguished breath of her son.

Elisha wastes no time. Giving Gehazi his staff, Elisha instructs him to run ahead: "Lay my staff on the face of the child" (v. 29). But this attempt at miracle fails: "There was no sound or sign of life" (v. 31). The woman and the prophet finally catch up to Gehazi at the house, and the servant is forced to admit, "The child has not awakened" (v. 31).

At this dreadful pronouncement, "Elisha went in and shut the door behind the two of them and prayed to the LORD" (v. 33). (And maybe, just maybe, there is happily ever after in the kingdom of God?)

That day, in the village of Shunem, Elisha stands at the bedside of miracle. The boy's eyes flutter open. He draws a deep breath. A grieving mother receives back her dead son. We behold this as the preliminary event to a future day—when God would lose his son and gain him back. There would be incredible heartache and disbelief in the days intervening Jesus' death and resurrection. Where was God? Why had he stood idly by when Jesus had been arrested on false accusations and crucified because of cowardice? "We had hoped that he was the one to redeem Israel," his disciples had lamented (Luke 24:21). It was a moment of utter perplexity and confusion. And yet it was not the final scene.

The Christian story, centered as it is on the death and resurrection of Jesus Christ, is the only story for making sense of desire and loss. Not all is right

> *The Christian story is the only story for making sense of desire and loss.*

with the world, this world. But our story isn't over yet. More will be written. And the resurrection of Jesus Christ is like a seed of hope sown into our stories of despair: it's the opening chapter of the new creation, where death and disease, sin and suffering promise to be reversed; where beauty and hope—life—will one day be renewed. This is reason to desire: to pray boldly and to believe that God wants to do good in the world, even if that good fails to be fully realized now.

In her book *When God Talks Back,* psychological anthropologist T. M. Luhrmann sets out to explain how sensible people believe in an immaterial God. One aspect of evangelical Christianity that she finds particularly compelling is its promise of joy, and Luhrmann talks about the theme of ultimate joy found in the stories of Tolkien and Lewis. She cites from an essay of Tolkien's:

> The consolation of fairy-stories, the joy of the happy ending . . . a sudden and miraculous grace . . . it does not deny the existence . . . of sorrow and failure: the possibility of these is necessary to the joy of deliverance; it denies (in the face of much evidence, if you will) universal defeat and in so far is evangelium, giving a fleeting glimpse of Joy, Joy beyond the walls of the world, poignant as grief.[11]

Our Father. The Bible nudges us toward the risk of wanting in a world that slowly leaks with disappointment. It challenges us to hold fast to the doctrine of God's goodness when life, like a reckless child, stubbornly heads in the direction of the street. Most of us will sit down to dinner, and life as we know it will end.

And that will be our occasion—for faith.

§

Stomach cancer. She has two months to live, my nephew tells me. My husband and I are driving to church, and I receive this impossible news in numb silence. It is February when we learn of Jimmy's mother's terminal diagnosis, and she is dead and buried before Easter, just two months shy of my nephew's high school graduation.

We attend the funeral. We try and make ourselves believe that the blond-haired boy whose childhood has already been sufficiently tragic is now orphaned.

Jimmy is alone. And he is not. Home has been pre-arranged for him by the kind providence of God. Six months earlier, God had inspired in me the desire to bring my nephew to Canada to live with us. And in this way, God was proving himself to be "Father of the fatherless and protector of widows . . . in his holy habitation. God settles the solitary in a home. . . . Blessed be the Lord" (Psalm 68:5-6, 19). Losing his mother has been an unimaginable cruelty for my nephew. But mercy had somehow sidled alongside.

We want. Life leaks. Desires are disappointed. And God, our Father, remains eternally good.

> *We want. Life leaks. Desires are disappointed. And God, our Father, remains eternally good.*

Reflection Questions

1. What Scriptures nudge your own heart toward believing that, despite your sideways scenes, God is good and loves you infinitely?

2. What desires are you unwilling to risk with God because of potential loss?

3. What might you stand to lose if you ignore those desires?

6

The Business of Holy

Prayer

I learn that I am pregnant—and cannot pray. This is not my surprise pregnancy with the twins, although I don't pray then either. It is a year earlier. In less than two weeks' time, my husband and I will be leaving our three young children to accompany a team of medical professionals to Africa. We have been vaccinated before our missions' trip with a bevy of inoculations I would never have otherwise needed: Hepatitis (the range of the alphabet), yellow fever, tetanus, oral anti-malarial pills. Every time I am seated beside a nurse holding a large syringe and she asks me, *Are you pregnant?* I assure her I am not.

I am. And I don't discover this until the immunizations have done the damage I am now powerless to undo. I suspect the pregnancy for a week. But if I don't take the test and fail to confirm the pregnancy, it cannot be true. Eventually this wildly ridiculous reasoning gives way. I buy a test. I take it. The line colors red.

It's the blood draining from my face.

Immediately, I call my friend from our church small group who is an obstetrics and gynecological resident at a teaching hospital in Chicago. Over the phone I deliver a panicked story—vaccinations, pregnant—and wait for the words of incantation that reverse the pox

I've put on this baby. I want her to reassure me that everything will be fine. But she answers me in a sensible doctor-voice, a voice I don't recognize. "What's done is done. You can't worry about what has already taken place." I worry nonetheless. I am undone by the worry.

Before we hang up, my friend schedules me for an ultrasound, and several days later, I arrive at the hospital, dread lodged somewhere deep in my uterus alongside the baby I have unwittingly though irreversibly damaged. It is a long walk from the parking garage through the glass corridors and up to the obstetrical floor, and I shuffle my steps, reluctant to arrive, hesitant to have news. I want to turn around and pretend away my nightmare of these waking hours.

I arrive. I undress. There is an awkward intimacy in the moment where I lay naked on the table, naked with fear. A screen illuminates. It shows pixilated shots of amorphous fetal tissue. We sit together in the expectant silence of that dark room, and my friend remains deaf to my inaudible questions: Will the baby live? Live normally?

Back in her small resident's office, outfitted with a desk and a bed, I sit down. She sits next to me. Her eyes meet mine, and I discover there fears of her own.

"Normally, I wouldn't tell my patients this," she says, "but something doesn't look right."

I begin to cry. Instantaneously, it's as if I am wedged into a constricting space. I cannot pray what I want. I cannot want what I should pray.

"How do I pray, Holly?" I ask her. "How can I say, *God, save this baby*, when I am not sure that's what I really mean and want? And how can I *not* pray for God to save this baby and wish for the alternative?"

"Jen, this is when you pray, *'Your will be done.'*"

I fall into her arms sobbing. Days later, I miscarry.

One year later, I am pregnant again. I cannot pray. This time, there is no fear that I have harmed the baby, and still, I don't want it. I want to go to graduate school. And do not meet the notion of my surprise pregnancy as equitably as Mary, mother of God, when the angel Gabriel delivers her news. "I am the servant of the Lord; let it be to me according to your word," Mary had said (Luke 1:38). I throw no conspicuous spiritual tantrum, just fling silence at the sky.

I don't pray until many weeks later—on the day I find myself lying on another ultrasound table in another hospital. It's on this day that I hear the technician reassure me soothingly that I'll "see my babies soon." And standing on the precipice of that surprise and looking down into the chasm of the unknown, my tongue is loosed. I break my silence. *I break.* And pray another version of the prayer I had prayed one year earlier.

"Father, whatever it is that you have decided to give, we embrace."

Canon of Confusion

We can't do away with a sense of struggle in the Christian life. Struggle is biblical, and authentic desire is often rooted in struggle. Although one familiar maxim of the Christian faith implies otherwise (*God's Word says it, I believe it, that settles it*), struggle is inherent to the tangled tensions of faith. Often we find ourselves in situations that don't immediately seem desirable: a surprise pregnancy, as an example, or singleness or childlessness or unemployment or divorce. *Struggle* is an apt word for describing what happens in between the moments when God meets us with these unwanted surprises and we relent to his goodness—between *God's Word says it* and *I believe it.* Struggle, in fact, is prerequisite to surrender because it necessarily signals that a battle has raged before the raising of a white flag.

> *Struggle is prerequisite to surrender.*

If it were true that struggle, even desire, was of no estimation in the life of faith, if all that mattered to God was obedience, no matter how mechanical, we would have an abridged version of the Scriptures. We could eliminate all the red-blooded men and women who want and pray—men like Abraham, women like Hannah. We could strike from our canon the stories of men and women who struggled to make sense of God's call, and didn't, at least initially, want to follow. And while we're at it, we could do away with the confusion of the Garden of Gethsemane where the Son of God struggled to bear the enormity of surrender, where he prayed with the desire that God remove from him the cup of suffering (see Matthew 26:36-46).

Like it or not, the inspired Scriptures tell these impossibly human stories. These men and women look a lot like us. Their willingness and their wanting to do the will of God never arrived fully assembled. Their life was the making sense of the space between *God's Word says it* and *I believe it*. They struggled to bear the weight of God's sovereignty and to call it good, just as we do.

In fact, it seems clear that one of the only things we should learn to expect in our life with God is surprise (and struggle). There's probably no clearer biblical narrative of surprise than the story of Abraham, whom God called to "go . . . to the land that I will show you" (Genesis 12:1). This can hardly be considered a call of particular clarity. Abram subsisted on meager details about how God meant to fulfill his promises of land and family.

Although God tells Abram that his offspring will be as numerous "as the dust of the earth," between the biblical record of chapters 12–14 in Genesis, a time span that surely occupies more years than it does pages, God intervenes with no words of reassuring guidance or clarification. Only after Abram voices his growing despair that his servant Eliezer will be heir does God interject to promise Abram a biological son (Genesis 15:4).

This would have seemed an opportune time to clear up the issue of maternity, but God is again silent, leaving it to Abram to walk into the mess of taking rival wife, Hagar, into his bed and producing a son, Ishmael, who promises to be "a wild donkey of a man, his hand against everyone and everyone's hand against him" (Genesis 16:12). Only later does God affirm that the promised heir will also be Sarah's offspring (Genesis 17:16), at which point the suggestion seems so outrageous as to produce outright laughter (Genesis 17:17).

If these major omissions weren't proof enough of what would seem God's reckless abandon to Abraham's potentially missing his plans and purposes, we might also mention that when God first calls Abram to leave familiarity behind and go to a strange land, he leaves out the inconvenient and messy details of the rites of circumcision, which he will later require of all the male members of Abraham's household.

Why all this deliberate obscurity? Why does God seem to prefer to leave Abraham to moments of obvious doubt, even despair? Wasn't this unnecessarily cruel? Could God not have spared Abraham the difficulties, the missteps, and provided instead a clearer blueprint of his intended methods?

> *Clarity and certainty are not the soil in which faith grows.*

But clarity and certainty are not the soil in which faith grows, and had Abraham had more advance notice from God, he may never have become the man whose faith was credited to him as righteousness, a faith that was honest enough to admit to God his doubts yet resilient enough to wait on divine timing. "And without faith it is impossible to please him, for whoever would draw near to God must believe that he exists and that he rewards those who seek him" (Hebrews 11:6). We please God not by gymnastic feats of pious religion; we please him as we begin actively trusting, in the midst of our struggle, that he is good.

The psalmist affirms that God's word is a "lamp to [our] feet and a light to [our] path" (Psalm 119:105), reminding himself (and us) that, like Abraham, we will receive no more light, no more knowledge, no more certainty than is required for our very next step of faith. What is faith if not a series of hesitating steps forward? What is faith but feeling our way in the proverbial dark, unclear about the direction we're taking, uncertain about the purpose behind the divine imperative? What is faith but the willingness to believe and act on the smallest, faintest perception of God's voice and the divine nudge from behind? What is faith but the enormous risk of relinquishing the guarantees of certainty? These are the kinds of questions that challenge us to examine our desires and expose their real nature. Have we trusted—or have we demanded control?

Prayer is a means of bringing our authentic self to God and meeting him in these mysteries. We pray because we hope and believe that surrender can be forged there, on our knees. We pray because sometimes this is all we can do when desire and the undesirable have us knotted inside. We pray because, when the woods have gone dark, when the distance between *God's Word says it* and *I believe it* feels like impossible terrain to travel and our only companions are doubt and fear, we need words as simple as these: *Your will be done.*

Humanity Untucked

Prayer is the courageous act of bringing our authentic desires before God. Prayer is the place where, in Jesus' name, we meet a holy God with all of our humanity hanging out. In our bravest moments of unscripted, unedited prayer, we find ourselves telling God what we want, how we're afraid to want this, how we fear he'll withhold, how we fail to trust and to worship and to reverence. We allow ourselves to see—and be seen. In this struggle, prayerful and raw, we willingly wait for the mercies of God to deliver us into the abiding belief that he is good. Prayer, bold and beautiful and brave, takes on the quality of our struggle to surrender to the God who is holy, to the God whose holiness produces our surprise.

This kind of prayer is courageous because as we pray, we enter the throne room of God, just as Isaiah did in Isaiah 6. As happened to Isaiah, one glimpse of holiness can produce knee-knocking terror. "Woe is me! For I am lost; for I am a man of unclean lips, and I dwell in the midst of a people of unclean lips; for my eyes have seen the King, the LORD of hosts!" (v. 5). The threads of Isaiah's humanity unravel and fall into a clumsy, ugly heap. Standing painfully aware of the gap lying between human and holy, his own reflection in the mirror undoes him.

This is the double vision of prayer: we see God and we see ourselves. This is also the double vision of holy desire. As those redeemed in Christ, we begin wanting holiness, yet recognize that our desires continue in the qualities of being human. Saved though we are, we bring to our desires a limited range of understanding. We want from God and yet fail to grasp the height, depth, breadth and width of God's holy purposes for our lives and for the world. We are growing in goodness and yet are capable of persisting in myopic selfishness: like Isaiah, we face this uncleanness, see this ugliness.

Holy desire is formed in the throne room. We have to see God rightly and understand that holiness is not a trifle. It is awesome. It is terrifying. It will undo us. It will not suffer the greed and impatience and mistrust of unholy desire. And it will also commission us. "Whom shall I send, and who will go for us?" (v. 8). Holy desire will be conscripted. We will be put to work. To pray in the throne room of God is take up a willingness to be sent.

"In contrast to Uzziah, who went to the temple to *use* The Holy for his own purposes, Isaiah was in the temple to pray and to worship. He wasn't there to get something for himself," writes Eugene Peterson, "but to be present to the Presence."[1] Peterson is noting a difference standing between unholy and holy desire: our attitude toward the Holy. When we approach God with unholy confidence, believing that he can be coerced into granting our good (as we define it), we are not in the throne room. We are in our living room.

Keeping Broomstick Straight

The cross of Jesus Christ is fundamental to this business of desire. We don't ever grow up from the cross, don't ever graduate from the fundamental truth that prayer and faith, desire and obedience hang suspended on the eternal certainty of God's love and forgiveness demonstrated for us at the cross, where God pierced the hands and feet of his son, *the lamb of God, who takes away the sins of the world* (John 1:29). We, as sinful, selfish beings, can want freely and yet boldly enter the throne room because of the cross. We can want from God because he—the Holy—has wanted us.

Like Mary Karr's *K* in her poem "Revelations in the Key of K," the cross keeps us "broomstick straight."[2] Our posture is grace. The cross makes a paternity claim—that we are children

> *We can want from God because he—the Holy—has wanted us.*

of God and privy to inheritance because we've been adopted. When Jesus teaches us to pray *Our Father*, it's an audacious dare. We take it up because of God's severe mercy displayed at the cross on our behalf. "In Romans 5 and 8, drawing together the threads of the argument so far, [Paul] says that the cross of Jesus reveals supremely the *love* of God (5:6-11, 8:31-39)," writes N. T. Wright. "Because the gospel reveals this covenant love, this covenant faithfulness of the living God, Paul knows that whatever happens the future is secure. . . . The death and resurrection of Jesus have unveiled the faithful love of God, and nothing can separate him from it (Rom. 8:38, 39)."[3] The cross is the certainty that God loves us and wants to hear from us. We are secure in God's love because of the cross. The cross is an invitation to come to the Holy without pretense—untucked, unscripted and struggling to surrender.

In his book *Mere Christianity*, C. S. Lewis teaches that the opening address of the Lord's Prayer—*Our Father in heaven*—announces that "the Christ Himself, the Son of God . . . is actually at your side and is at that moment beginning to turn your pretence into reality. . . . You are dressing up as Christ."[4] Prayer is a way we play at our privileges as eldest sons. Romans 8 details the rich inheritance and intimacy with God that is ours to enjoy because our adoption papers have been signed and sealed in the blood of Jesus. Christ met the moral requirements of the law, freeing us from the enslaving power of self-love. Christ made himself poor, guaranteeing us the riches of heaven. The Christ who appealed before his death to his Abba Father has given us the same confidence with which to approach God.

Daddy! Prayer in the name of Jesus Christ allows us to endear God and believe that we are endeared to him, despite the obvious obstacles of our sin and struggle. Our Father readies a welcome for us like the father in the parable of the prodigal son. Though God has every reason to hold against us the record of our wrongdoing, though he has every right to recall the occasions when we've borne against him—the Holy—a sense of entitlement, though his is the prerogative to remind us that we are elder brothers, haughty and self-righteous who wish to place God in our debt, he is faithful. He does not call to mind our faithlessness. He reserves the best of robes for the worst of sinners. He throws parties for prodigals and celebrates the lost come home. He divides his inheritance among the undeserving. "All that is mine is yours!" (Luke 15:31). At the cross, the Father forgives his unfaithful sons and daughters.

Our Father. The God to whom we address our prayers and petitions has limitless generosity and a bottomless appetite for doing good. His reflexive impulse is to bless, and his blessings are not just for those who seem, at least superficially, to deserve it. In fact, he delights in blessing those who seem most out of reach of grace: the tax collector and the prostitute, the criminal and the leper. He blesses the diseased and the downtrodden, the beggar and the blind. At the cross, the Father demonstrates fully the lengths to which he will go to love humanity: To degradation. To death. We can want from this God.

Though the cross is an event to follow the Lord's Prayer canonically, it is an important reason the words Jesus taught us to pray are so rudely elementary. *Our Father, holy is your name. Give us this day, lead us not, deliver us.* This prayer that lacks theological ornamentation and religious elegance, this prayer that suffers a childlike quality about it—it can be so bare because Jesus took on human flesh, with all of its vulnerabilities and needs, and became a sufficient sacrifice.

We have a demonstration of the antithesis of the humble simplicity of the Lord's Prayer in 1 Kings 18, when Elijah confronts Ahab and the prophets of Baal. Elijah proposes a test for finding out who is the true God of Israel: he and the false prophets will each tend to their own altars and will call upon their gods to set fire to their offerings. "You call upon the name of your god, and I will call upon the name of the LORD," says Elijah to the 450 prophets of Baal and the 400 prophets of Asherah gathered at Mount Carmel. "The God who answers by fire, he is God" (v. 24).

The prophets of Baal spend their day in frenzied prayer. They cry out loudly. They dance circles around the altar. They cut themselves, as if letting blood were required for moving god. Elijah taunts them. "Cry aloud, for he is a god. Either he is musing, or he is relieving himself, or he is on a journey, or perhaps he is asleep and must be awakened" (v. 27). But nothing works. Baal's offerings are stone cold.

Figuring Baal's prophets recognize their defeat, Elijah calls for water. Four jars. Four more. Twelve jars in total. The offerings to Yahweh are thoroughly soaked, and the trench Elijah has built around the altar is filled to overflowing. In the face of that impossibility, Elijah prays. "O LORD, God of Abraham, Isaac, and Israel, let it be known this day that you are God in Israel, and that I am your servant, and that I have done all these things at your word. Answer me, O LORD, answer me, that this people may know that you, O LORD, are God, and that you have turned their hearts back" (vv. 36-37). One simple repetition—*answer me*. The only insistence here is on the character of God and the desires of God.

Fire falls. "The prayer of a righteous person has great power as it is working," James wrote, referring to Elijah. We know that righteousness found its supreme expression in the God-Man Jesus Christ.

Simplicity in prayer works because of the grace of the gospel. Desire in prayer works because of the cross. There are no linguistic hoops through which to jump to make our prayers palatable to God. Indeed, if prayer depended on our holiness, the privilege would be immediately revoked. Rather, prayer depends on Jesus, who has opened to us the way to the Father. He entered the womb of Mary, submitted to the baptism of John, reclaimed the role of the temple for himself. This Jesus has thrown open the doors of heaven, pitched his tent among us and given his life to usher us into the throne room of grace. Jesus, our advocate, brother and friend intercedes on our behalf. It is by the blood of Jesus Christ that we pray and are heard, and it is in the righteous name of Jesus Christ that we find the confidence to believe our prayers are heeded by the Ancient of Days, who has judged our sin through Christ and allowed him to bear on his shoulders "the chastisement that brought us peace" (Isaiah 53:5). Before the God-Man, we can come untucked. And we, the unholy, can be made to want.

> *Desire, expressed in prayer, risks on grace.*

Practice of Grace

Eugene Peterson has said this about grace: "In fifty years of being a pastor, my most difficult assignment continues to be the task of developing a sense about the people I serve of the soul-transforming implications of grace—a comprehensive, foundational reorientation from living anxiously by my wits and muscle to living effortlessly in the world of God's active presence. The prevailing North American culture . . . is . . . a context of persistent denial of grace."[5] As we resist grace, we also resist prayer. Dependence on God unnerves us, and we are profoundly unsettled by our insufficiencies. What if God doesn't manage my life as efficiently and effectively as I? What if he doesn't care to?

Desire, expressed in prayer, risks on grace. Is this too bold of us? Is our hope in the real effectiveness of prayer warranted by God's character?

Jesus convincingly portrays God as patient, generous and compassionate. The Gospel of Mark seems to especially emphasize Jesus' sympathetic heart gripped by love for those in need. Mark tells us Jesus is "moved with pity" (1:41), is "grieved" (3:5), and feels profound compassion for the crowds who "were like sheep without a shepherd" (6:34). Chapter after chapter, scene after scene, Jesus is tireless in his love. And although throngs of people hound and hassle Jesus and stand waiting presumptively at every shore at which he disembarks, Jesus is an eternally patient man. He wills interruptions for the sake of the sick, the lame, the blind, the demon-possessed.

"If you will, you can make me clean," says the leper to Jesus.

"I will; be clean," Jesus responds (Mark 1:40-41).

In the Gospels, people approach Jesus with endless self-interested requests, and we could say that their desires are akin to prayers. I don't intend to puzzle out the mechanics of prayer here in this book. I'm quite happy to let the theologians untangle the theological knots. (Does it change God? Does it simply change me?) But I can't resist what seems to be a common-sense reading of the Scriptures: when people pray, things happen. Abraham prays: Lot is spared. Isaac prays: Rebekah conceives. Jacob prays: Esau reconciles. Joshua prays: the sun stands still. Gideon prays: the fleece is wet. Hannah prays: Samuel is born.

Whatever prayer is, it is real participation with God. "God does indeed allow Himself to be decided by prayer to do what He otherwise would not have done," wrote Andrew Murray. God likes to be asked, says Richard Forster. "He is not deaf, he listens; more than that, he acts," insisted Karl Barth. "He does not act in the same way whether we pray or not. Prayer exerts an influence upon God's action, even upon His existence. That is what the word 'answer' means." C. S. Lewis put it this way: "The scene and the general outline of the story is fixed by the author but certain minor details are left for the actors to improvise. It may be a mystery why He should have allowed us to cause real events at all; but is it not odder that He should allow us to cause them by prayer than by any other method?" These theological thinkers may or may not have accurately described prayer, but at least they're wrestling with the inherent tensions of involving ourselves in conversations with God.[6]

Of course, not all prayer is answered in the manner requested, and this shouldn't come as a surprise either. It is, after all, participation in the *holy*. David prays that his illegitimate son, to whom Bathsheba has given birth, will recover. The baby dies. Paul prays three times for relief from the "thorn in his flesh." God refuses. "My grace is sufficient for you, for my power is made perfect in weakness" (2 Corinthians 12:9). Jesus prays for his cup of suffering to pass: "My Father, if it be possible, let this cup pass from me" (Matthew 26:37). But it does not, for he must drink it down to its bloody dregs.

Prayer, in fact, is never only about getting what we want from God. It is a bold invitation to meet with God in our authentic human experience, which is to say doubt and desire, praise and perplexity, fear and failure. Prayer cannot pretend. It calls us out of our proverbial hiding and into the light. And day is a brilliant beginning for spiritual transformation.

Take No Care: Learn to Praise

I initially meet the necessity of writing this chapter on prayer in a loathsome state of despair. I have absolutely no ink of insight to fill these pages on prayer. I have only wordlessness. *Help me, God*, I pray—and believe. It's the following morning when my yearly Bible-reading plan serendipitously takes me to the opening scene of 1 Samuel. Hannah is praying for a son.

Year after year, Elkanah has been dutifully reporting to Shiloh for the obligatory sacrifices. Year after year, he has been bringing with him his two wives, Peninnah and Hannah. Peninnah comes with children: she is the mother of a large brood. Although the Scriptures don't tell us how many children she had, we know she had enough to provoke disdain of and lord superiority over her rival wife, Hannah. Penninah's verbal cruelty becomes a tradition with the sacrifices: "So it went on year by year. As often as she went up to the house of the LORD, [Penninah] used to provoke [Hannah]" (1 Samuel 1:7).

Elkanah loves his wife Hannah and tries to make up for her barrenness (and Penninah's verbal abuse) by giving her a double portion to offer to the Lord. "Hannah, why do you weep? And why do you not eat? And why is your heart sad? Am I not more to you than ten sons?" he asks tenderly, albeit naively (v. 8). But his generosity, even his goodness to her as a husband, does not soothe her distress. In agony, Hannah cries out to the Lord.

> O LORD of hosts, if you will indeed look on the affliction of your servant and remember me and not forget your servant, but will give to your servant a son, then I will give him to the LORD all the days of his life, and no razor shall touch his head. (1 Samuel 1:11)

Hannah desires a child, and we can suppose that she has long wanted one. In this particular scene, the thrashing desire undignifies prayer. Eli, the priest, takes Hannah for a drunken woman because he catches sight of her weeping. She is moving her lips, although no sound is issuing. "How long will you go on being drunk? Put your wine away from you," he says to her (v. 14).

Hannah's long unrequited desire for a child had left her in an embittered state of soul. It hardly seems fitting that she should pray. But then again, why shouldn't she pray? Wouldn't the invitation of grace seem to say that all are welcome at the throne of grace (Hebrews 4:14-16)? That prayer begins at the point of authenticity? And that, even if it is anger, doubt and disappointment with God, praying those sentiments is better than not praying at all?

In *Lit*, Mary Karr recounts the writing advice she receives in a letter from Toby Wolff, author of *This Boy's Life*: "Don't approach

your history as something to be shaken for its cautionary fruit. . . .
Tell your stories, and your story will be revealed. . . . Don't be afraid
of appearing angry, small-minded, obtuse, mean, immoral, amoral,
calculating or anything else. Take no care for your dignity."[7]

This writing advice can also apply to prayer: *take no care for your
dignity*. Brave is the only way to write, and brave is the only way to
pray. Neither is clean and bloodless. Yet the untucked prayers—the
prayers of our struggle—prepare the way for surrender, even praise.
Many of the psalms have this unedited quality I am suggesting and
trace the arduous journey between struggle and praise.

> The prayers of
> our struggle prepare
> the way for surrender,
> even praise.

"Why, O LORD, do you stand far
away? Why do you hide yourself in
times of trouble?" (Psalm 10:1). The
psalmist sees the unchecked arrogance
of the wicked, who "boasts of the desires of his soul . . . and renounces the
LORD" (v. 3). The psalmist opens with an assertion of his doubt. He
is troubled by God's apparent unwillingness to intervene on behalf
of the helpless, for whom the wicked "lurks in ambush like a lion
in his thicket" (v. 9).

"Forget not the afflicted!" he cries out (v. 12).

In the process of courageously admitting to God what he considers
to be his divine shortcomings, the psalmist's doubt actually begins to
erode. "But you do see, for you note mischief and vexation, that you
may take it into your hands; to you the helpless commits himself; you
have been the helper of the fatherless" (v. 14). He nudges himself back
toward remembering what is true about God. And although the in-
justice he has seen and cried out against still stands, he eventually
surrenders himself again to the mysterious goodness of God.

As the psalm bears out, surrender will evolve organically into
prayers of praise. "The LORD is king forever and ever; . . . O LORD,
you hear the desire of the afflicted; you will strengthen their heart;
you will incline your ear to do justice to the fatherless and the op-

pressed" (vv. 16-18).

By the grace of Jesus Christ, struggle has the potential to become surrender, surrender to become praise: this is the gospel chain of cause and effect. Struggle challenges me to trust, but when I do eventually surrender, it means I've entrusted my life to God. And every time I do this, I'm heartened by the knowledge that God is eternally capable. The Lord's Prayer does not offer explicit thanksgiving or praise to God, but I realize now how impossible it would be to trust God and address him as "Our Father" without inspiring the knowledge that he has loved us eternally and freely—which is, of course, a truth that can make a heart sing.

Prayer that becomes praise: and this is proof that God is becoming our desire.

❧

He leaves wet on my lips. Slipping his backpack off of his shoulders, handing me a fistful of crumpled papers and an empty lunchbox, he starts to dash off to the playground.

"Wait!" I call after him, watching his legs clumsily halt mid-rotation. "Where's my kiss?"

He comes back dutifully, smiling and willing to hand over the payment I exact for nearly every maternal task I am asked to carry out on his behalf. Snack? A kiss. Help reaching something on a closet shelf? A kiss. Carrying your backpack and lunchbox and crude drawings of Jango Fett? A kiss.

He leaves wet on my lips and then disappears around the corner of the school building. I call after his twin brother, who is faster and has already disappeared from sight. I am left imbalanced under the load of what belongs to both of them and what they should rightfully be carrying.

I am left with wet on my lips.

And suddenly I am swept into the days when I will not so easily cajole my sons into kissing me, when they will disappear into adulthood and leave me feeling imbalanced—with fewer things to carry and still the desire to do so.

I love this life: me, the mother of this brood of children. I would no longer wish away the plan God visited upon me unsuspecting and unwilling nearly six years ago when I was told I would "see my babies soon." There were years of struggle to embrace this providence. There were moments I could not pray. In truth, I have often failed to call it sweet.

But on this day, when I am left standing in the middle of a playground, I feel gratitude rise in my throat. I feel praise forming on my lips.

God, thank you for this.

Thank you for wet on my lips.

Reflection Questions

1. When have you stood in the space between *God's Word says it* and *I believe it*?

2. How would your prayers change if, in the presence of the Holy, you took no care for your dignity?

3. In what current struggle do you wish you could more easily pray, "Father, whatever it is that you have decided to give, I embrace"?

7

Bread and Butter

Petition

I notice the hot pink socks, the swollen ankles. She is wearing a wool sweater, and the July sun is bearing mercilessly down on the café umbrellas that shade this busy street running through Montreal, on her vagrant pals congregating at the corner.

I hope she's not a regular.

We have just arrived in Montreal and parked our car behind the building where we've rented a flat for a month. As we round the corner from the alley, I see her sitting there on the stoop of a vacant building, holding her head in her hands. Her long, grey hair hangs like a shroud, though not obscuring her coal-black eyes and eyebrows penciled in cynicism.

I hope she's not a regular. This is my immediate thought, loathsome though it may be, but I want in no way to feel responsible for a homeless woman this summer when I'm supposed to be finishing a book proposal. If I am forced to pass her every day on this stoop, the woman with misery in her hands, this is exactly how I will feel: responsible.

Three consecutive days I pass her sitting on the stoop. I choose to say nothing. The mercury of July is rising, and every day she is dressed in her wool sweater and hot pink socks, her capri jeans clinging tightly to her stout legs. On day four, I decide that I will have to make necessary acquaintance with the woman in the hot pink socks. Despite all my cheerful optimism, she is clearly a regular.

After I've dropped the kids off at summer camp and parked the van in the back of our building, I round the corner like I've done every day for the better part of a week. She is there, as I expect her to be.

"Hi," I start. "I've just noticed you the past couple of days and thought we should say hello. What's your name?"

She stares at me blankly. "Why?"

Her question hangs in the air. It taunts my naiveté. Realizing I've begun stupidly, I try again. "I see you here most days, and because I'm always walking by, I just thought I could introduce myself and be friendly. I'm Jen."

I stick my hand out to shake hers.

She gives me her hand, and I shake it. She never gives me her name, and our conversation ends just as awkwardly as it has begun. I turn to leave and walk toward the laundromat/café where I will spend the day writing. What makes a woman learn to doubt the motives of the world? What pain leaves a woman with her head in her hands and bags at her feet? What heartache wears wool in July? I consider these sincere questions—and feel sincerely compassionate. It's also true that while pink socks and I see each other nearly every day and we smile and chat briefly, life continues cheerfully for me. We form no real friendship, and I remain comfortably withdrawn from whatever sadness has brought her to the front stoop of the building three doors down.

Give us this day our daily bread.

The urgency of this request is lost on me. I am a have in a have-not world. I wake to clean water running from my faucet. I have multiple toilets that flush. The nearest hospital is minutes from my house, and the neighborhood where I live is safe. We have two cars, two refrigerators, and when it is winter, all seven of us leave our house in goose-down coats. In the summer, we afford the luxury of keeping cool.

I haven't ever needed to worry about how we would pay for groceries or keep the electricity from being shut off. When one of our children outgrows a bicycle, we buy a new one. When a school fee is due, we pay it. When the co-pay for one of our children's surgeries registers two hundred dollars, I don't decide what necessity we'll temporarily live without.

Give us this day our daily bread.

I am a have in a have-not world. I often wonder how I am to learn this prayer, which was essentially, in Jesus' day, a prayer for beggars. Only the poorest of the poor begged daily rations of bread. Only those at the lowest economic rung of society had to suffer this daily indignity of soliciting human good will. When Jesus tells his disciples to ask for their daily bread, he's identifying them with the least of the least. This is something I find great difficulty in doing: me, a fat North American cat.

There's obviously something about petition for earthly needs that is meant to humble us. In asking for God's provision, we're admitting our inability to self-

> *In asking for God's provision, we're admitting our inability to self-sustain.*

sustain. We can't live independently of him. We need help. Maybe this is why so few of us pray, or why prayer makes us so profoundly uncomfortable, or why it serves as a last resort when we find ourselves in a bind. We like living by the myth of our superpowers. We get what we need, working and trying hard. We work hard at the working and trying. Isn't this meritocracy at its best?

But the petition of the Lord's Prayer—*give us this day our daily bread*—is a prayer for rich and poor alike. For the poor, they are betting that if God rained bread from heaven in the past, he can do it again; that if the God of the universe feeds the birds, surely he can feed me. It dares them to believe that he wants to. This is a prayer to confirm what the Bible tells us about God—that hunger matters to him who takes up the cause of the widow and the fatherless and the immigrant, all of the most economically vulnerable in ancient times. I want the poor of the world to pray this prayer. I want them fed by Jehoveh Jireh, the God who provides.

But I also want rich people like me to pray it too, because it is altogether too easy to withdraw from those in greatest need, to forget that God meets the needs of the world through his church—*through me*. These words may be the way we learn to live into the holy desire to give and give up. These words may be the way we move beyond the habits of luxury and incremental accumulation. These may become the words for determining our tortured choices— choices between give and keep.

And if all the haves of the world prayed, *Give us this day our daily bread*? Would we see beyond pink socks and thick ankles into humanity's face? Would we "not . . . be haughty, nor . . . set [our] hopes on the uncertainty of riches, but on God, who richly provides us with everything to enjoy"? Would we "do good, . . . be rich in good works, . . . be generous and ready to share, thus storing up treasure for [ourselves] as a good foundation for the future, so that [we] may take hold of that which is truly life" (1 Timothy 6:17-19)? I am a have. And I want God's liberal and compassionate generosity for the have-nots. This is one desire formed in me as I pray for daily bread.

Manna

In the biblical text, food has physical and spiritual significance, and the meal is often the place where heaven and earth meet. In the Old Testament, for example, the worship of God's people was embedded in their food traditions. The multiple feasts they celebrated throughout the year were not only occasion for gathering to remember the goodness of God and to offer sacrifices for honoring him; they were also reasons to eat.

Families, in certain instances, were fed at God's table. When they offered fellowship or peace offerings (these were the most common sacrifices) in order to give thanks, to fulfill a vow or as a freewill offering, they ate what was left from the portion of food they first offered to the Lord (Leviticus 7:11-18). As well, priests ate a portion of each household's sin, guilt and grain offerings (Leviticus 2:3, 10; 6:26). As the Israelites presented lambs and doves, grain and new wine, they recounted the stories of God's provision. They also feasted. The "pleasing aroma" of worship offerings wasn't just the spiritual fragrance of human obedience. It was more material than the "sacrifice of praise," which the writer of Hebrews solicits from his readers. It was also the smell of roasted lamb (Exodus 12).

These worship rituals differ substantially from our contemporary ones, especially in my evangelical tradition, where congregants stand shoulder to shoulder, sing hymns, drop change into the offering baskets, and then sit subdued as someone stands and preaches. Unless there is robust emphasis on the Eucharist (or Communion, or the Lord's Supper, as one prefers to call it), the entire service passes for a weekly theological download—a very different experience than the multi-sensory experience of the Old Testament feasts or even today's Catholic mass, which engages the body and the senses.

Food is an important metaphor throughout the Scriptures. But food wasn't only metaphor, as if its only purpose were symbolic. For example, bread, biblically speaking, is also calories—by it our bodies are fed and sustained. When the Israelites left Egypt (and with it, their diets of cucumber, melons, leeks, onions and garlic, Numbers 11:4-6), God fed his wandering people with the bread of heaven. Every morning except for the Sabbath, they awoke to "a fine, flake-like thing, fine as frost on the ground. . . . It was like coriander seed, white, and the taste of it was like wafers made with honey" (Exodus 16:14, 31). When the nation of Israel left Egypt in haste, they could not take with them sufficient provisions of water and food for the journey. They had to abandon themselves to the risk of faith and trust that God would be faithful. This wasn't just a spiritual proposition. Their breath depended on it.

The manna God gave was intended for a dual purpose. It was sustenance in both the physical and the spiritual sense. Manna was supposed to be the reassuring sign that the Israelites could count on God to provide for all their appetites. "He humbled you and let you hunger and fed you with manna, which you did not know, nor did your fathers know, that he might make you know that man does not live by bread alone, but man lives by every word that comes from the mouth of the LORD" (Deuteronomy 8:3). We shouldn't miss that the writer of the Pentateuch is saying something altogether strange here: God fed the people physically in order to make them spiritually hungry.

Unfortunately, the Israelites were, in ways similar to us, an obtuse people. Although the provision of manna in the wilderness was miraculously and lovingly provided by God, the Israelites complained with great regularity about the bread from heaven. They wanted meat and pined for the produce of Egypt. "There is nothing at all but this manna to look at!" (Numbers 11:6). All too often, the Israelites' failure to love and trust God was most obvious at mealtime.

Psalm 78 tells the tale of ancient Israelite whining. "They tested God in their heart by demanding the food they craved. They spoke against God, saying, 'Can God spread a table in the wilderness? He struck the rock so that water gushed out and streams overflowed. Can he also give bread or provide meat for his people?" (vv. 18-20).

But their sin was obviously greater than the guilt of picky-eating: "They did not believe in God and did not trust his saving power" (v. 22). Scripture clearly tells us that God was feeding his people bread not only to keep them alive but to communicate profound spiritual truth: *men and women hunger for God, and God is capable of feeding them.* The Israelites' inability to gratefully receive God's provision of manna amounted to a rejection of God. They failed to grasp the spiritual lesson of the manna—

that physical bread alone never satisfies human hunger.

Spiritual hunger is an undeniable biblical theme. Jesus was especially eager to emphasize the spiritually hungry condition of the human heart. In the wilderness before he begins his public ministry, Jesus is tempted by Satan to turn stones into bread. Jesus resists Satan, reciting the Scripture he'd learned as a child when memorizing the Hebrew Torah: "Man shall not live by bread alone, but by every word that comes from the mouth of God" (Matthew 4:4). When John records in his Gospel the strange interaction Jesus has at midday with a Samaritan woman, he notes that the purpose for their layover in this Samaritan village was for the disciples to buy food. But when they returned with the food, Jesus didn't immediately eat. "I have food to eat that you do not know about," said Jesus, referring to his work of proclaiming the kingdom of God (John 4:32). After Jesus fed the five thousand and the crowds tailed him to the other side of the lake, he rebukes them, saying, "Truly, truly, I say to you, you are seeking me, not because you saw signs, but because you ate your fill of the loaves. Do not work for the food that perishes, but for the food that endures to eternal life" (John 6:26-27). Later in the sermon, Jesus identifies himself as that eternal food. "I am the bread of life; whoever comes to me shall not hunger, and whoever believes in me shall never thirst" (John 6:35).

But an important question remains, one especially significant for our discussion about desire. Is it fair to conclude that physical bread and physical appetite are ultimately less important to God than spiritual bread and spiritual appetite? Is this the lesson that the manna was meant to teach? And as it relates to our discussion here in this book, does this point to a deeper truth about desire? Should we pay little attention to our earthly appetites and focus instead on "spiritual" ones? Are the holiest people those who learn to self-forget, who've mastered the secret of needing nothing and wanting nothing? Are we wrong to pray about the spectrum of our earthly needs and desires?

It's true that God means to move us into rhythms of contentment.

Paul describes in Philippians 4:11-12: "I have learned in whatever situation I am to be content. I know how to be brought low, and I know how to abound. In any and every circumstance, I have learned the secret of facing plenty and hunger, abundance and need." We are blessed when we meet lack with an attitude of abundance, when we praise rather than complain, when we cheerfully receive however little or much God has provided. Were we to learn and practice the virtues of contentment and abide, in the sense of being deeply satisfied in and by God whatever our material circumstances, we would glorify the sufficiency of Jesus Christ. This, in a world disquieted by discontent, would be beautiful.

> We are bodies, with bodily needs, and those needs matter to God.

However, it is also true that needing God and asking God for one's needs is hardly selfish. The lesson of the manna is that God gives bread to feed both our bodies and our souls. *Give us this day our daily bread* is petition that positions us for reliance and dependence on God. It reminds us that we are bodies, with bodily needs, and invites us to begin believing that those needs matter to God.

Do not be anxious, saying, "What shall we eat?" or "What shall we drink?" or "What shall we wear?" For the Gentiles seek after all these things, and your heavenly Father knows that you need them all. But seek first the kingdom of God and his righteousness, and all these things will be added to you. (Matthew 6:31-33)

Give us this day our daily bread forces us back into our bodies and explodes the way we try and elevate the spiritual over and above the earthly. Asking for bread can certainly mean, *Feed me spiritually, Lord.* It can also fundamentally mean, *Can I get some dinner, God?* There is an invitation in the request for daily bread to solicit God for our everyday, earthly needs.

Yes, satisfy us, God, with yourself. And let us also eat.

Gnostic Fantasies (and Fallacies)

Gnosticism is a heretical worldview that has been plaguing Christianity since its first-century origins. Gnostics (or Neo-Platonists) divided the world into two distinct realms: the visible, material world and the invisible, spiritual one. According to their dichotomy, materiality itself was evil. Gnostics believed that a person made spiritual progress by releasing attachment from the physical world (and earthly concerns) in exchange for spiritual priorities and a higher *gnosis*, or knowledge. For this reason, Gnostics disavowed the incarnation of God in the man Jesus Christ. They did not believe that God could take a material body, for this would have been an act of betrayal to his purity.

It is not difficult to see how many Scripture verses could be twisted to lend themselves to an essentially Gnostic misinterpretation. "If then you have been raised with Christ, seek the things that are above, where Christ is, seated at the right hand of God. Set your minds on things that are above, not on things that are on earth. For you have died, and your life is hidden with Christ in God" (Colossians 3:1-3). We could easily read this verse as an injunction to reject our "earthly" life in favor of our "heavenly" one. We could construct our own Gnostic dichotomy, rendering everything material as lesser, even evil. This would easily forbid us from praying for earthly desires.

As Christians, it is right for us to want to pursue the "first things" of God's kingdom. But how do we know when our desires aren't distractions from the real business of God's kingdom coming, especially when they feel so crassly human and earthly as wanting a home, a car, a job, a spouse? How we do know our petitions aren't greedy tactics of North American entitlement and the insistent wanting for more? How do we recognize sly maneuvers of selfishness that mask themselves as prayer? These are good questions to ask about desire, but they do not demand that we eviscerate prayer and forbid the act of asking. We would have to agree that prayer without petition feels hollowed out, seeming more like pretense than the sincere trusting act it is meant to be. We have needs and wants, and to try to eliminate these from prayer in an effort to be more "spiritual" is gnostic, even cowardly. We have to make a better way forward.

> We have needs and wants, and to try to eliminate these from prayer in an effort to be more "spiritual" is gnostic, even cowardly.

G. K. Chesterton, the British writer and Christian apologist, defends the goodness of desire in his book *The Everlasting Man*. In one section, he compares Buddhism's and Christianity's solutions to evil desire. Buddha proposed we get rid of desire altogether and considered it a contagion against which we must be inoculated. Chesterton argues that the Christian gospel does not obligate us to give up on our desires but rather to judge their nature:

> [Buddha] proposed a way of escaping from all this recurrent sorrow; and that was simply by getting rid of the delusion that is called desire. It was emphatically *not* that we should get what we want better by restraining our impatience for it, or that we should get it in a better way or in a better world. It was emphatically that we should leave off wanting it. . . . The Buddhists call this beatitude. . . . Certainly to us, it is not indistinguishable from despair.[1]

"I do not see, for instance," Chesterton argued, "why the disappointment of desire should not apply as much to the most benevolent desires as to the most selfish ones."

Augustine, like Chesterton, suggests this same kind of introspective, biblically guided process. William Cavanaugh writes, "In Augustine's thought, we desperately need not to be left to the tyranny of our own wills. The key to true freedom is not just following whatever desires we happen to have but cultivating the right desires."[2] Sin, said Augustine, is "the immoderate urge towards those things at the bottom end of the scale of good [whereby] we abandon the higher and supreme goods, that is you, Lord God, and your truth and your law."[3] The Bible insists on the doctrine of sin and its sly substitutions—but it doesn't take up the Gnostic project of reneging on desire.

❧

We were moving back to Chicago for Ryan to attend graduate school. I was pregnant with our third child and anxious to be settled into a home that could accommodate the needs of our growing family. But because we were moving from Columbus, Ohio, we were certain to pay more for less in the Chicago suburbs. It seemed impossible to hope for certain things in a house.

And yet I prayed—boldly and specifically. I still have the piece of lined paper on which I recorded the requests I made of God in advance of our move. There was the inventory of more suitably spiritual requests: for more opportunities to write, for the discipleship ministry I was leaving behind, for a new church home, "a place to grow and serve." But there were also specific requests for a house: for a house in the right location at the right price. For office space, a play room and two full bathrooms—"an added bonus," as I noted in my prayer journal.

We got that house.

And when I retold this story several years later to a group of young moms from my church, one woman remarked snidely, "So you can pray for the house of your dreams and get it?"

I didn't mean to say exactly that.

❧

In the Gospel of Luke, there is a particular emphasis on the feast. Luke records nineteen feasts, thirteen of which are exclusive to his Gospel. And as the events surrounding Jesus' crucifixion and resurrection are detailed, three meals are referenced: the Passover meal, which Jesus shares with his disciples before he is betrayed; the meal shared by the disciples and the resurrected Jesus in the village Emmaus; and a third meal with more disciples, where Jesus, in an effort to prove that he is a resurrected man and no mere ghost, asks for something to eat. Either the disciples were a particularly gluttonous bunch, or the New Testament feast, like the Israelite feasts, was prescriptive of Christian faith and practice.

The Scriptures actually tell us that Jesus "was known to them in the breaking of the bread" (Luke 24:35). Perhaps this is because Jesus asked them to remember him in the physical acts of eating and drinking. "He took bread, and when he had given thanks, he broke it and gave it to them, saying, 'this is my body.' . . . And likewise the cup after they had eaten, saying, 'This cup that is poured out for you is the new covenant in my blood'" (Luke 22:19-20). Why did Jesus choose to memorialize himself in such a material way? Why not let Scripture itself stand sufficient for narrating the events of his life, death, burial, resurrection and coming return?

Because we are *bodies*, and the lessons we often best absorb are the ones we learn with our senses. Last winter, I read Kathleen Norris's marvelous little essay "The Quotidian Mysteries: Laundry, Liturgy, and Women's Work." After a long hiatus from spiritual commitment, Norris explains how she made a return to her childhood faith, relating her experience at a wedding mass as she watched the priest prepare the Eucharist and afterward, clean the dishes of the sacred meal. The ritual "welcomed me, a stranger. . . . Eating and drinking were something I could understand. That and the housework."

Extraordinarily, Norris was invited into the church and into faith by a domestic act serving as a metaphor—by a meal. A meal is so unbelievably material. It is not the means of spiritual epiphany that we are used to expecting. And a meal, by its very nature, reminds me that God may ask me to tend to my abstractions less and to incarnate myself more: to be present in the breaking of bread, to feast, to remember him in the bread and the wine, and to look forward to the day when the church will be seated at his eternal table of love. The meal makes me present in my body and family, in my community and church. The meal gives me skin and challenges my long-held Gnostic distinctions, the very ones that have forcibly kept me from attending to my desires. I am tempted to reject anything that feels "earthly" in favor of what feels "spiritual." I pit devotion against desire because it feels necessary to my spirit-body dichotomy. I think it's often true that I reject desire because I reject the meal—and reject my own body and the sense that I exist in this world in a way that is temporal and physical.

Norris reminds us beautifully of the lessons we learn seated at our tables. "Each day brings with it not only the necessity of eating but the renewal of our love of and in God. This may sound like a simple thing, but it is not easy to maintain faith, hope or love in the everyday. I wonder if this is because human pride, and particularly a preoccupation with intellectual, artistic or spiritual matters, can provide a convenient way to ignore our ordinary, daily, bodily needs."[4]

Give us this day our daily bread: here is an invitation to admit to God that we have earthly needs. We live in bodies—and bodies need food, shelter and sleep. God knows this,

> We live in bodies—and bodies need food, shelter and sleep.

understands this and condescends compassionately to our humanness: "He knows our frame; he remembers that we are dust" (Psalm 103:14). Asking for bread—and physical, earthly needs—can be holy prayer indeed.

N. T. Wright, in his book *The Lord and His Prayer*, explains that

> at the heart of [his prayer for daily bread] stood a central biblical symbol of the kingdom: the great festive banquet, which God has prepared for his people. . . . The whole point of the Kingdom . . . isn't about shifting our wants and desires

on to a non-physical level, moving away from the earthly to the supposedly "spiritual." It is about God's dimension coming to birth within ours. . . . The Kingdom is to come *in earth as it is in heaven.* Daily needs and desires point beyond themselves, to God's promise of the kingdom in which death and sorrow will be no more. But that means, too, that the promise of the Kingdom *includes* those needs, and doesn't look down on them sneeringly as somehow second-rate.[5]

Wright concludes, "Those who feel deeply threatened by God knowing all our desires will naturally want the Lord's Prayer to be about 'spiritual issues.' If I'm ashamed of my desires, and would prefer God *not* to know them, then it will be much more comfortable for me if the 'daily bread' for which I pray is for the soul, rather than the stomach."[6] Wright points out that Gnosticism in the context of desire has much to say about our fear. We don't want to own our earthly desires because we are afraid of what they will say about the state of our soul.

Requisitions

I've always felt like praying the Lord's Prayer was risky business. Dare we pray for the coming of God's kingdom and the doing of God's will? Aren't we inviting such cataclysmic change into our spiritual weather patterns that the only end result can be storm? Won't it challenge us to lay down many of our desires and to begin praying differently?

Yes. I think that's exactly the danger of praying the Lord's Prayer. Maybe it's the reason we hold it at arms' length. We are conflicted about the extent to which we want to be formed in the desires of God. How much will I have to give up? How much will it cost? Which of my desires will I have to surrender in exchange for the priorities of God? Frederick Buechner said it this way in his book *Whistling in the Dark*:

We do well not to pray [the Lord's Prayer] lightly. It takes guts to pray it at all. . . . "Thy kingdom come . . . on earth" is what we are saying. And if that were suddenly to happen, what then? What would stand and what would fall? Who would be welcomed in and who would be thrown the Hell out? Which if any of our most precious visions of what God is and of what human beings are would prove to be more or less on the mark and which would turn out to be phony as three-dollar bills? Boldness indeed. To speak those words is to invite the tiger out of the cage, to unleash a power that makes atomic power look like a warm breeze.[7]

To pray this prayer is to step into something powerful and to draw near to someone untamable. Why, then, does the power of prayer, to which Buechner refers and to which the Bible testifies, seem like it frequently fails to fully materialize, that is, if I measure it by the standard of my own prayers? Why does prayer lack substantial impact in my life? I pray, and it's business as usual. Why?

We are afraid to pray as boldly as the Lord's Prayer invites us to pray. Our prayers are meek. We expect so little of God. Our petitions are hesitant, and our courage for asking God and expecting answers falters. Can we be so bold as to name what we want? Isn't that like bursting into the throne room waving a stack of requisitions?

Some would tell us that specifically naming what we need and want in prayer is wrong. In researching this chapter, I was reading about Jesus' first miracle (turning the water into wine at the wedding in Cana) from a commentary on the book of John. The author explains why it was that Mary approached Jesus with the wine shortage.

> *We are afraid to pray as boldly as the Lord's Prayer invites us to pray.*

Mary's sharing her dilemma with Jesus was possibly a habit bred of long years of family dependence, in the apparent ab-

sence of Joseph (Mk. 6:3). Her request, essentially informing
him of the need, is a helpful model of *intercessory prayer.* (*Cf.*
11:3, 'the one you love is sick'; 2 Ki. 19:14.) We all have a
tendency to use prayer to dictate to God. Our part is to lay the
need before him, and then trust him to respond as he wills.[8]

The author interprets that we pray best when we sketch for God the
barest generalities of our needs. We shouldn't presume to suggest
the best way of meeting those needs—that's God's job.

If he is correct, wouldn't the Lord's Prayer assert the state of need
(*We're hungry*) rather than naming the request (*Give us this day our
daily bread*)? But of course it doesn't. It is as bold to suggest that we
tell God the ways we want him to meet our needs. I understand the
hesitation this author has about prayer (and *desire*) that degrades
into childishness. *I want what I want when I want it, and I want it
right now!* We should be wary of telling God what to do and stay
attentive to the greed that simmers below the soul's surface. And
we should, as the apostle Paul teaches, lay our requests before God
as we simultaneously thank God for what he's already given and
how he'll choose to answer (Philippians 4:6). But we cannot cease
to ask, not if we want to remain faithful to the model of prayer and
desire that the Lord's Prayer builds.

Metamorphosis

N. T. Wright talks about the way petition, as formed by the Lord's
Prayer, changes. "If we linger here, we may find our priorities
quietly turned inside out. The contents may remain; the order will
change. With that change, we move at last from paranoia to prayer,
from fuss to faith." Wright continues:

> The Lord's Prayer is designed to help us make this change: a
> change of priority, not a change of content. This prayer doesn't
> pretend that pain and hunger aren't real. Some religions say
> that; Jesus didn't. This prayer doesn't use the greatness and

majesty of God to belittle the human plight. Some religions do that; Jesus didn't. This prayer starts by addressing God intimately and lovingly, as "Father"—*and* by bowing before his greatness and majesty. If you can hold those two together, you're already on the way to understanding what Christianity is all about.

Finally, he concludes, "The danger with the prayer for bread is that we get there too soon."[9]

One biblical character whose life evidences the tension and transformation of desire is Jacob, the man who wrestles God for his blessing. His namesake means "he takes by the heel" or "he cheats" (Genesis 25:26). And Jacob does both, causing great consternation to his mother, Rebekah, when he and his brother, Esau, tussle violently in the womb. Jacob is born physically grasping his brother's heel, and he grows into the man who grasps at everything else his brother has: his birthright, which, at an opportune moment, he persuades his brother to sell for a bowl of stew; his blessing, which, at the behest of his mother, he connives from his blind father by posing as Esau. When his practices of deception meet the murderous rage of his brother, he flees the country.

On his way out of town, Jacob meets God. One night, he lies down to sleep and begins dreaming that he sees angels ascending and descending from heaven. He hears the voice of God, and God promises him the blessings of Abraham. "Surely the LORD is in this place!" Jacob says when he awakens, astounded (Genesis 28:16).

But lest we think that Jacob's heart is given to sincere worship, listen to his terms of agreement: "If God will be with me and will keep me in this way that I go, and will give me bread to eat and clothing to wear, so that I come again to my father's house in peace, then the LORD shall be my God" (Genesis 28:20-21). This was still the cheater Jacob, with no more elemental motivator than self-interest.

It is over the course of the next twenty years that we see him change. Jacob has formerly always been the one to do the cheating, but as a member of his uncle Laban's household, he is the one who is cheated. He is given Leah when he has worked for Rachel. When he has been promised the speckled and spotted livestock as wages, they are cunningly removed from the herds. Finally, twenty years later, after having lost complete faith in Laban, Jacob and his household pack their bags and decide to return home to the land promised to Abraham.

But the Jacob we meet on the return trip is altogether altered from his former self. In Genesis 32, Jacob prepares to meet his brother, Esau, whose anger he can only hope has been assuaged with the passing of time. However, when Jacob learns that Esau is traveling in the company of four hundred men, he struggles to hope. He strategizes, divides his household and prepares for attack.

But he also prays:

> O God of my father Abraham and God of my father Isaac, O LORD who said to me, "Return to your country and to your kindred, that I may do you good," I am not worthy of the least of all the deeds of steadfast love and all the faithfulness that you have shown to your servant. . . . Please deliver me from the hand of my brother. . . . You said, "I will surely do you good." (Genesis 32:9-12)

Notice that the prayer is petition: there is a very definite request that Jacob makes of God. *Please deliver me from the hand of my brother.* But he does not negotiate with God or insist on making some crass exchange for divine help. For the first time, we may see Jacob appraise himself realistically. *I am not worthy.* Is Jacob finally owning up to his character as a liar and cheat? Does he stand ready to read the record of his moral debt? Has he come to understand the scope of his sinfulness? And is this because he is beginning to understand God rightly?

All these acknowledgments matter in the transaction of trust that desire and, ultimately, prayer require: if we are to come to God asking and asking well, we must understand first that we do not deserve to receive. God is not in our debt. Desire that gets corrupted emerges from a heart of demand: *I want this and should have it because I deserve it.* But this isn't Jacob's attitude. He manages to petition God without petulance, although he maintains stubborn faith in the promises of God. This inspires his desire and request. *Save me from my brother because you have promised to do me good.*

> God is not in our debt.

This transformation that occurred in Jacob is the change God intends for each of us. Holiness will re-form us: it will reshape the way that we view ourselves as well as the way that we view God. It will change the way that we pray because it will revise our personal desires. It will even change the ways that we most fundamentally understand our identity: "Your name is Jacob; no longer shall your name be called Jacob, but Israel shall be your name" (Genesis 35:10). But in the midst of the metamorphosis of desire, we can yet cling to the confidence that God issues the invitation to *ask*.

Give us this day our daily bread.

❧

I picked up the neighborhood newspaper and opened to the real estate roundtable. Predictions were, said the realtors confidently, that, although the condo market could potentially cool, demand for single-family homes in Toronto would continue to increase. While housing prices were sinking in the United States, they were climbing steadily in Toronto. Our pastor and his wife had bought into the Toronto market nearly eight years ago, and since that time, their house has nearly doubled in worth. The median home price in Toronto now nears $800,000.

Ryan and I have often talked about whether or not we feel confident praying for a house to buy in Toronto. Years ago, I had boldly and confidently prayed for a house in the Chicago suburbs with two bathrooms, office space and a play room, and despite someone's suggestion that this had been a crassly materialistic prayer, we both believed God had answered it. And yet, I was having more difficulty praying this prayer in Toronto.

Maybe I have been coming to understand, to a greater degree, what it means to be a have. Although it is not wrong to make money, only to love and trust in it, I am the first to admit that wealth does not usually afford the perspective for measuring the degree to which we love it and trust in it. If we can buy what we need when we need it, can we judge ourselves impartial to that perceived security? I could say that I don't love money, but I wouldn't really know if that were true. I could defend that I'm not greedy by detailing what we give and give away. But I don't dare. "The heart is deceitful above all things and beyond cure. Who can understand it?" (Jeremiah 17:9 NIV). Maybe it's this that gives me pause.

I remain open for God to grant me the willingness to pray for a home here in Toronto, a willingness I do not now have. I recognize that in the desire for a home, there can be a godly desire for rootedness and for place. This is the desire I feel willing to cultivate, and maybe I will one day confidently begin praying for a home in Toronto. Not yet.

When God sent his people into exile in Babylon, he gave them this command: "Build houses and live in them; plant gardens and eat their produce. Take wives and have sons and daughters. . . . Multiply there, and do not decrease. But seek the welfare of the city where I have sent you into exile and pray to the LORD on its behalf, for in its welfare you will find your welfare" (Jeremiah 29:5-7). This is the text our pastor preached this past fall, and he used it to call those of us who rent in the city to consider buying. Make this your *home*, he pleaded.

I want to pray this. I want to move beyond my suspicions about materiality and overcome my Gnostic misunderstandings, and I believe that our desire to live in Toronto is oriented toward the desire for God's kingdom. But still, I fear greed. I recognize the contradictions of my desires. Maybe these are not to be done away with, at least not in this lifetime.

But by grace, it's a lifetime I have to learn to pray this: *Give us this day our daily bread.*

Reflection Questions

1. Do you easily pray for material wants and needs? Why or why not?

2. What might it look like, in your own life, to reconcile an attitude of contentment with the practice of petition?

3. If you could be so bold as to suggest to God how he meet your needs, what would you begin asking of him?

8

If the Shoe Fits

Confession

Colin and Andrew are buzzing around the playground after school, chasing their playmates and forming trains on the slide, at the bottom of which they fall into giggly heaps of tangled arms and legs. They are ecstatically happy on this June afternoon, which cheerily announces that school is almost finished and summer days will soon be here to stay. But then Andrew dumps the entire bag of crackers I have packed for him and comes running to me, crying.

"Well, if you're going to run around the playground with your bag open," I answer, "you're going to spill your snack!"

Between the noise of his shudders and sobs, my unsympathetic speech is lost. Meanwhile, his classmate is meticulously piling the spilled crackers up for easy scooping and disposing, a plan that seems not only compassionate but brilliant. Then someone's foot pulverizes the pile. The sobs begin anew.

"Don't worry, sweetie," I reassure Andrew. "We have more crackers at home." And this finally consoles him despite the obvious disappointments of the empty bag and the mutilated cracker pile. He rejoins his brother, and they disappear to a corner of the school play yard, obscured from view.

Minutes later, I learn that one of them has been fighting over a soccer ball with another little boy. I approach the mother of said victim. Her little boy cowers tearfully behind her legs, and when I ask what has happened, she admits there's been a tussle. But it hasn't only been that.

"Michael says your son spit on him when they were fighting over the ball."

Like all ad hoc moments of motherhood when we're confronted with egregious crimes of our children, I am faced with two choices: melt, like the Wicked Witch of the West, into a steamy mass of mortification, or find my son and make him apologize. Mother of five, twelve years of experience under my belt: I choose the former.

The twins have, by now, climbed to the top of one of the playground's laddered structures. I find the spitter.

"Get down here."

Something about my inflexible tone communicates the need for punctilious obedience because he doesn't even argue. ("I love your mom voice, Jen," my friend Janey has often told me. I suspect I'm using it here.)

"Did you spit on Michael?"

"No!" he insists, shaking his head. His eyes avert my gaze.

"I want you to tell the truth," I remind him.

He finally nods, his eyes widening. *Yes.*

Truth is a big fish. A mother must be strong at the reel.

"You'll need to admit to Michael what you've done wrong and ask for his forgiveness," I say, rehearsing our family rituals of confession.

The spitter follows me obediently and does as I have asked him. I kneel to mediate the plea bargain, hoping it will smooth the tearfully ruffled feathers of the other little boy and his mom. And because five-year-olds have memories like chalkboards, the injuries are quickly erased and forgotten. Amends come mercifully easy, and the boys run off together to play.

"I wasn't sure I should have told you," the other mother admits sheepishly. "I'm just not always sure how to handle these things."

She looks at me as if for advice, figuring that I've seen this a time or two before.

"No, I'm absolutely glad you did. My husband and I want to teach our children that when they do wrong things, they need to admit what they've done, apologize and ask for forgiveness."

It's the simplest life lesson. If only we all had mastered it in kindergarten.

Habits of Grace and Truth

Forgive us our sins. The Lord's Prayer teaches us to wear the habit of truth telling, and I hope this book has reflected a commitment to candor. While I have wanted to identify ways that my theology of desire has been found wanting and to correct the assumption that desire is categorically sinful, I have also wanted to admit that our desires are easily corrupted because of sin. We, too, are found wanting. This truth about desire is a tightrope we walk.

I realize how it can feel like an impossible bind. And it would be, except for grace. Though selfishness cannot be wrested from the heart with self-effort, God can achieve this work by his methodical, merciful grace. We don't plot or predict grace. It is operative in ways that are clandestine. Indeed, as Ruth Haley Barton writes in the introduction to her book *Sacred Rhythms,* there is so little of our own maturity and growth that we actually superintend. "I cannot transform myself, or anyone else for that matter. What I can do is create the conditions in which spiritual transformation can take place, by developing and maintaining a rhythm of spiritual practices that keep me open and available to God."[1] We give grace accessibility to our hearts when we engage in intentional spiritual practices.

One important spiritual practice is the practice of confession. As Andy Crouch writes,

> As for Christians, well, we really have just one thing going for
> us. We have publicly declared . . . that we are desperately in

need of Another to give us his righteousness, to complete us, to live in us. We have publicly and flagrantly abandoned the project of self-justification that is at the heart of every person's compulsion to manage perceptions. . . . This means telling the world—before the world does its own investigative journalism—that we're not as bad as they think sometimes. We're worse. . . . If we're being honest about our own beauty and brokenness, the beautiful broken One will make himself known to our neighbors.[2]

Confession allows us to be the worst of sinners and yet remain confident that God is committed to us still. Holy desire is best paired with confession.

The Lord's Prayer invites us into confession and speaks sinner's much-needed language of grace. It reminds us that prayer does not have to be complicated. We don't have to be hung up on doing it right. God hears because Jesus is our high priest and makes a faithful intercession for us. *Grace* is one of the first words of faith. And confession, as a spiritual practice, thrives in an atmosphere of grace. Without grace, there is fear. And where there is fear, confession will be muted. Confession will always be unwelcome in places where authenticity engenders judgment and where we are pressured to conform and perform. Until we're allowed to be the mess we are, we will continue the hiding, the lying and the pretending. We will flee truth telling.

> *Confession allows us to be the worst of sinners and yet remain confident that God is committed to us still.*

However, when the gospel is the light that illuminates, we can betray the messy truth about ourselves. "Do you realize that it is only in the gospel of Jesus Christ that you get the verdict before the performance?" writes Tim Keller in *The Freedom of Self-Forgetfulness*. "In Christianity . . . God imputes Christ's perfect performance to us as if it were our own."[3] The gospel frees us from the desperate clutch of perfectionism. Only Jesus need be perfect. Because of the substitution that was made at the cross, we are no longer guilty, but innocent—and this of no merit of our own. Like the criminal beside whom Jesus was crucified, we hang guilty and powerless before our sentence of death. "Jesus, remember me when you come into your kingdom," the man had asked (Luke 23:42). Jesus forgives and frees. "Truly, I say to you, today you will be with me in Paradise" (v. 43). Every time we come to confession, we come to that naked moment of truth and receive from God the wildly improbable gift of grace.

Jesus once told a parable "to some who trusted in themselves that they were righteous, and treated others with contempt" (Luke 18:9-14). It was a story for those who felt they didn't need confession. The Pharisee and the publican enter the temple together. Both stop to pray. The Pharisee reads his curriculum vitae to God. "I thank you that I am not like other men, extortioners, unjust, adulterers, or even like this tax collector. I fast twice a week; I give tithes of all that I get" (vv. 11-12). He cites his consistent and reliable acts of moral virtue. He measures the paces between himself and *sinners*.

The publican—ill-reputed for lying and cheating, known for being willing to break another man's back to turn a profit—is, on the other hand, broken under the sanity of his own self-appraisal. "Standing far off, [he] would not even lift up his eyes to heaven, but beat his breast, saying, 'God, be merciful to me, a sinner!'" (v. 13). He does not detail his offenses, but guilt ricochets inside him, explodes through his consciousness with searing force, indicting both intention and action, thought and deed. He has not committed sins. He *is* a sinner.

One is justified; the other is not.

This parable Jesus tells is a parable about the humility required for truth telling. Confession, made possible by the innocent suffering of the One who came in grace and truth, is a way forward into our contradictions and the steady reassurance that, on the basis of Christ's willing sacrifice, God will never leave or forsake us.

We humble ourselves in our acts of confession, just as we've been commanded to do (see James 4:10). And what can we expect from God in response? He "gives grace to the humble" (James 4:6).

Wishful Blindness

Whether we're small children on the playground or big people with real jobs, we don't come easily to the practice of confession. Dan Ariely, professor of psychology and behavioral economics at Duke University, has authored a book, *The (Honest) Truth About Dishonesty*, in which he concludes that, rather than opting for the honest admission of their mistakes and moral failures, people lie— to themselves most of all.

In his research, Ariely sets out to test the prevailing theory of rational economics, which explains human dishonesty as a moral cost-benefit analysis. Rational economists say that we do our math before we cheat or lie. Will we get caught? And if we're caught, what will happen? When what we stand to potentially gain outweighs the probability of getting caught (or the consequences we'd incur if we were), we cheat, at least according to the Simple Model of Rational Crime, or SMORC.

Ariely's research, however, disproves this theory of human rationality. We aren't so well reasoned when temptation comes along. For example, we don't cheat disproportionately more when more stands to be gained. And we don't lie extravagantly more when we feel secure that our deception will never surface. Instead, "we cheat up to the level that allows us to retain our self-image as reasonably honest individuals," says Ariely.[4] We prefer to see ourselves as *bending* the rules, rather than *breaking* them.

The optimistic self-talk requires us to create persuasive justifications for our (albeit small) indiscretions. We minimize our failures. We tout our successes. We tell ourselves that *other* people are cheaters and liars. Here are some of the typical stories Ariely found that we tell ourselves in order to excuse our dishonesty:

- It's ok to cheat someone who has wronged us.

- It's less wrong to steal something that isn't actually money.

- It's acceptable to cheat in ways that are less deliberate or purposeful.

- If we're tired and morally taxed, a small indiscretion can be excused.

Ariely's research affirms that people generally want to be honest. We don't like to consider ourselves as outlaws. However, if cheating and lying are as prevalent as Ariely claims, we can't be as honest as we self-describe.

As a conclusion from his research, Ariely wants us to see that the moral perceptions that we have of ourselves aren't always reliable. "Remember your irrationality," he warns. "Remember your fallibility."[5] Ariely insists we're prone to overestimate our virtue and to underestimate our vice. "We generally believe that we have a privileged view of our own preferences and character, but in reality, we don't know ourselves that well."

Ariely's research findings are biblical. The Scriptures bear out that we don't like facing the inconvenient truths of our moral indiscretions. Hypocrisy is an ugly face, so we find different truths to tell ourselves. We learn to narrate stories that make us the heroes, not villains. Ariely says this may be more "wishful blindness" than deliberate dishonesty. It is mistruth either way.

Forgive us our sins. The Lord's Prayer is freedom from that spin.

Functional Atheism

Many of us live by the hopeful myth that the sins we don't confess might effectively slip God's notice. Years ago, I remember leading a Bible study and inviting the women to pray Psalm 139:23-24. "Search me, O God, and know my heart! Try me and know my thoughts! And see if there be any grievous way in me, and lead me in the way everlasting." One woman told me, "I don't dare pray that!" The thought of inviting God to examine her heart was an unsettling one, although, were she to really consider the truth of the matter, she'd be forced to admit that God was already intimately acquainted with all of its treacheries.

We all sometimes act like functional atheists, forgetting that God—the Ancient of Days—is present with us and that it is his prerogative to judge us. When our children were younger, I remember praying to become more conscious of God as witness to everything I did and said within the four walls of our home. How easily I rationalized my irritable, angry tone of voice with my children. Most disturbing was how rarely I used that voice when a friend and her children happened to be spending the morning with us. I prayed to live with the abiding sense that God was *watching*.

The answer to that prayer came at dinnertime when our oldest daughter, then four, sat coloring at the kitchen table as I prepared dinner and downloaded the events of the day with my husband. Ryan and I began arguing about something, and my voice was growing shrill as Audrey's eyes were growing wide.

Soon, Mommy was sounding horribly mean to Daddy. My daughter, looking up at me reproachfully, said, "Mommy, you aren't being tender-hearted with Daddy."

(How, I might ask, does the Holy Spirit cram his magnitude into such small bodies?)

God sees. God knows. To confess isn't to tell God anything he doesn't know. It's simply to agree with God on our wrong-doing and wrong-being: that we sin because we are sinners.

But we may least want to confess when, if such an agreement were reached, we'd be forced into relinquishing the sin we secretly cherish. Maybe we don't want confession to force repentance. Augustine is famous for his prayer of half-hearted confession: "Grant me chastity and continence. But not yet."[6]

> *To confess isn't to tell God anything he doesn't know. It's simply to agree with God on our wrong-doing and wrong-being: that we sin because we are sinners.*

The Whole Truth—and Nothing But

We shouldn't confess because our highest value is brokenness. As Megan Hill writes in *Christianity Today*, "Christ at work in me doesn't permit me to rest in my failure. . . . Grace covers. And it covers again and again. Thanks be to God. But if we stop there, as so many writers do, we are only telling half the story. . . . Grace covers my sin, and then it pushes me to be more like Christ."[7] The drive behind confession should not simply be the desire to admit my sin and relieve my conscience; the real motivation must be the will for holiness. Holiness can result from confession because speaking aloud our sin to another person is often the first step in beginning to hate it.

> Speaking aloud our sin to another person is often the first step in beginning to hate it.

What's wrong with me? This is a question we're all forced to answer, especially when we are faced with our failures held against the highest standards (or, as is more commonly my case, the lowest common denominator). Confession gives us language for understanding our incurable moral handicap. In his book *Reason for God,* Tim Keller explains why the language of sin is such hopeful vocabulary. He quotes from a sermon by Barbara Brown Taylor, which explores the freedom confession grants:

> Neither the language of medicine nor of law is adequate substitute for the language of [sin]. Contrary to the medical model, we are not entirely at the mercy of our maladies. The choice is to enter into the process of repentance. Contrary to the legal model, the essence of sin is not [primarily] the violation of laws but a wrecked relationship with God, one another, and the whole created order.[8]

Confession is founded upon realistic self-understanding. If we do not acknowledge the role we often play in our own brokenness, if we do not admit the infiltration of our own selfishness into the picture of moral failure, we will inevitably lay the responsibility at the feet of others. Every sin, every disaster, every broken relationship will be someone else's fault. *Forgive us our sins.* Finally, we have the words we need to shift blame where it belongs.

Me. I'm the problem.

I am not suggesting that we take blame that isn't ours. If we have been the victim of abuse in our families growing up or in our marriages, for example, blame belongs to another. To say that we are sinners isn't to say that we are always perpetrator and never victim. I wouldn't want women who've been wronged and violated to concede to those trolling voices of self-accusation. And there are less egregious ways that we are sinned against than abuse. (I've been married seventeen years now. I might have some examples.) We need neither ignore nor accept blame for the everyday wrongs we suffer in our families and friendships, even if they fail the standard of criminal. Relationships flourish when we can gently yet honestly help others to understand how they've hurt us. Confession doesn't eliminate the need for confrontation.

Still, confession is usually warranted. As my daughter told me today on the way to school, "I'm going to admit to my friends what I've done wrong. I think it will heal some of the brokenness." Confession is a practice best done regularly. Daily. Incrementally. *Forgive us our sins.* We say these words and enter into an eternal pact of transparency, not only with others (although this, too, should prove true as a result of this prayer) but most fundamentally with God. "Against you, you only, have I sinned and done what is evil in your sight" (Psalm 51:4). As we confess our sins, we're inviting God into the labyrinth of our hearts: see me, know me, examine me and find that I am wanting. In confession, we are pleading for clemency: show me mercy, God, for I am a sinner. We are allowing God to investigate our desires—to try, even indict them.

Transparency, before both God and others, can rescue us from the corrosive effects of sin. In literature, we may have no more powerful portrait of the slow death we die when we refuse transparency and deny our sin than Arthur Dimmesdale in Nathaniel Hawthorne's *The Scarlet Letter.*

Hester Prynne is an adulterer: she has given birth to a little girl who is not her husband's child. We do not immediately learn who her lover is, but we come steadily to suspect that it is the Reverend Arthur Dimmesdale. We suspect him because throughout the novel, we see him grow more and more physically frail. In sermons, he alludes to his moral worthlessness, but he does not specifically confess his crime, which accrues to him more and more admiration from his congregants. They interpret his humility as more evidence of his virtue. Dimmesdale becomes increasingly physically afflicted by the secret he keeps. At one point in the novel, when trying to force Hester to publicly confess the name of the man she's slept with, Dimmesdale begs her to do what he cannot.

> I charge thee to speak out the name of thy fellow-sinner and fellow-sufferer! Be not silent from any mistaken pity and tenderness for him; for, believe me, Hester, though he were to step down from a high place, and stand there beside thee, on thy pedestal of shame, yet better were it so, than to hide a guilty heart through life. What can thy silence do for him, except it tempt him—yea, compel him, as it were—to add hypocrisy to sin? Heaven hath granted thee an open ignominy, that thereby thou mayest work out an open triumph over the evil within thee, and the sorrow without. Take heed how thou deniest to him—who, perchance, hath not the courage to grasp it for himself—the bitter, but wholesome, cup that is presented to thy lips![9]

When David committed treachery (adultery with Bathsheba and the subsequent murder of her husband, Uriah), he admits how the act of keeping silent about his sin made him feel as if his "bones wasted away. . . . My strength was dried up as by the heat of summer" (Psalm 32:3-4). Health was only restored to David when he acknowledged his sin to God. "I did not cover up my iniquity; I said, 'I will confess my transgressions to the LORD'" (v. 5).

Confession does not purify us; it is Christ's blood that atones for our wrongdoing. But confession can restore us to a certain sense of moral equilibrium, which the Bible calls integrity. When Abimelech mistakenly takes Sarah, Abraham's wife, into his harem, thinking her to be Abraham's sister, he is warned by God in a dream: "Behold, you are a dead man because of the woman whom you have taken, for she is a man's wife" (Genesis 20:3). Having been lied to by Abraham, Abimelech defends himself. "Did he not himself say to me, 'She is my sister'? And she herself said, 'He is my brother.' In the integrity of my heart and the innocence of my hands I have done this" (v. 5).

Integrity is the principle of oneness: the private self and the public person are the same. A person of integrity does not affirm principles by which he does not himself abide. Integrity means a person practices what she preaches. But since none of us is capable of perfectly practicing what we vehemently preach, and because this has the effect of splintering us into two selves (the self we *want* to be and the self we *are*), confession is a means to restoring us to truth. We cannot repair all the damage we do, but at least we can admit *that* we do it—without rationalization or excuse.

Perhaps the greatest reason to confess our sin to God is that this ushers us into his grace. There is no gospel—no *good news*—apart from the knowledge that we are sinners unable to rescue ourselves. If our misdeeds could be corrected by trying harder, we wouldn't need the blood of Jesus Christ to flow. We could rely on our own promises, rather than on the atonement.

Confession is the means by which we recognize it is Christ who breaks the power of sin. *Forgive us our sins.* We say these words and touch the wound of his side and hands, remembering that though sin exacts punishment, severe and eternal, we are spared because of the cross.

Have mercy on me, a sinner.

Foils and Foibles

Saul and David are fascinating Old Testament characters. First and second kings of Israel, these men represent the best and worst of what it means to be human. Both men end up screwing it up royally, although the consequences of their sin seem to differ vastly. Saul, impatient for the arrival of the prophet Samuel after he fails to arrive on the day he has promised, offers an unlawful sacrifice before going into battle. Furthermore, when commanded to annihilate the Amalekites, Saul fails to do so, keeping alive the king as well as the best of the livestock. As a result of his sin, the kingdom is torn from his hands. "Because you have rejected the word of the LORD, he has also rejected you from being king" (1 Samuel 15:23).

David, Saul's successor, sins in ways that seem more egregious than Saul's. Although he is called a man after God's own heart, he takes into his bed another man's wife, gets her pregnant, and tries to conceal the adultery by calling the woman's husband home from battle and inciting him to sleep with his wife. When this man, Uriah, refuses as a matter of principle, David resorts to murder, and when the news is reported back that his murderous plan has been successful, David reacts with terrifying callousness. "Do not let this matter displease you, for the sword devours now one and now another" (2 Samuel 11:25).

David, like Saul, suffers consequences for his sin (the baby's death and his son Absalom's rebellion), but God never reneges on his promise to eternally establish David's throne (see 2 Samuel 7:16). Why? Wouldn't David's sin seem grosser than Saul's? Saul's sin seems to be more a matter of degree than of kind: he offered the sacrifice when that was really Samuel's job. Later, he refused to destroy *all* the Amalekite herds. We know the reproof Samuel gives ("To obey is better than sacrifice," 1 Samuel 15:22), but it is still difficult to reconcile ourselves to the apparent inequity of punishment, especially when David's sin seems so much more flagrant and destructive than Saul's.

It's impossible to quantitatively measure sin and assign to any particular one a value. We can't say that one sin is greater and another less. But maybe a clue into God's handling of Saul and David and their individual acts of disobedience can be found in their relative willingness and unwillingness to acknowledge their sin *as sin*. Maybe their *confessions* (or refusals) offer a window into their hearts and to what extent they were devoted to God.

Saul's life is clearly built around the principles of expediency. He does what he deems necessary, and this actually prevents him from recognizing his actions as sin. They don't feel wrong; they feel necessary. When he offers the unlawful sacrifice on the eve of the battle with the Philistines, he finds four convenient rationalizations for his actions. "The people were scattering from me." "You [Samuel] did not come within the days appointed." "The Philistines had mustered at Michmash." "I [had] not sought the favor of the LORD" (1 Samuel 13:11-12).

Having convinced himself of the inevitability of his choices, Saul defends them. We see this no more clearly than when Samuel confronts him after the battle with the Amalekites. "Blessed be you to the LORD," he enthusiastically greets Samuel. "I have performed the commandment of the LORD" (1 Samuel 15:13). Samuel immediately asks about the bleating of Amalekite sheep, the lowing of Amalekite oxen. How can Saul say that he has obeyed the Lord when the evidence of his betrayal has been corralled in a pen?

Saul admits they had spared some of the animals for sacrifices. "[But] the rest we have devoted to destruction" (v. 15).

"Stop!" says Samuel. "Why then did you not obey the voice of the LORD?" (vv. 16, 19). He does not want to entertain Saul's excuses.

For the third time, Saul persists in stubborn self-defense. "I have obeyed the voice of the LORD. I have gone on the mission on which the LORD sent me. I have brought Agag the king of Amalek, and I have devoted the Amalekites to destruction. But the *people* took of the spoil, sheep and oxen, the best of the things devoted to destruction, to sacrifice to the LORD your God in Gilgal" (vv. 20-21). Saul shifts the blame, remaining recalcitrant.

Saul doesn't want to admit his guilt, not least because it threatens his honor, which he holds in higher regard than God's. Even when he finally does confess, he's motivated by crass self-interest. "I have sinned, for I have transgressed the commandment of the LORD and your words, because I feared the people. . . . Now therefore, please pardon my sin and return with me. . . . I have sinned; yet honor me now before the elders of my people and before Israel" (1 Samuel 15:24-25, 30).

Unlike Saul, David comes more readily to the act of confession. He is well prepared for confession, in fact, because his entire life has been a rehearsal of the reverent fear of the Lord.

When Saul is yet alive, David is anointed as the next king of Israel, inspiring Saul's plans to kill him. Even before he ascends the throne, he is a young man of courage. In 1 Samuel 17, his father sends him to take food to his older brothers, who are fighting in the Israelite army. He finds the king and his troops cowering in Goliath's shadow as he shouts menacing threats across the battle line. "Who is this uncircumcised Philistine, that he should defy the armies of the living God?" asks David (v. 26). David offers himself as a contender to fight Goliath.

David's fear of the Lord continues to serve as a covering of protection over him. In the wilderness of Engedi, David and his men hide from Saul in a cave, the very cave Saul decides to use as a makeshift latrine. David is urged by his men to kill Saul, but David refuses. "The LORD forbid that I should do this thing to my lord, the LORD's anointed, to put out my hand against him, seeing he is the LORD's anointed" (1 Samuel 24:6).

David spares Saul a second time in the wilderness of Ziph, where Saul and his army are encamped by night. Abishai and David steal into Saul's camp undetected, but David does not allow Abishai to kill Saul. "Do not destroy him, for who can put out his hand against the LORD's anointed and be guiltless? . . . The LORD forbid that I should put out my hand against the LORD's anointed" (1 Samuel 26:9, 11). Unlike Saul, David's highest value is not expediency.

In keeping with reverence, David is also a promise-keeper. Although it would have suited the cultural sensibility of David's day to annihilate every living relative of Saul after Saul's death in order to insure the security of his own throne, David was faithful to the oath he made to Saul's son, Jonathan. "Is there still anyone left of the house of Saul, that I may show him kindness for Jonathan's sake?" (2 Samuel 9:1). Mephibosheth, the lame son of Jonathan, is brought to the palace, and David insures that every day, he will feast with the king.

That David is a God-fearer is clearly apparent to those closest to him. In fact, his devotion to God inspires the contempt of one of his own wives (see 1 Chronicles 15:29). When David experiences rest from his enemies and Israel settles into a state of national security, David pledges to build a temple for God. "See now, I dwell in a house of cedar, but the ark of God dwells in a tent" (2 Samuel 7:2). The Psalter is filled with the songs of praise David composed for the God whom he loved and revered. He is a man who worships.

Yet for all of these exemplary qualities, David is no perfect man. He, too, is capable of great evil. David brings Bathsheba into his bed, and many months of impunity pass until the prophet Nathan confronts David. His is a treacherous act, as callous and cruel as the rich king who refuses to take a sheep from his own flock to prepare for his guest's dinner and instead pitilessly steals the one beloved lamb of his poor neighbor. This sin, before it is recognized as his own, incites David's fury. "As the LORD lives, the man who has done this deserves to die!" (2 Samuel 12:5).

"You are the man!" Nathan accuses.

It's in the next moment that we see the chasm between Saul and David. Both are guilty sinners. But David doesn't try to minimize or rationalize his sin as Saul had. When confronted by Nathan, he accepts full responsibility in a way in which Saul was never capable. "I have sinned against the LORD" (2 Samuel 12:13).

Confession requires few words: six to be exact.

Content of Confession

God is holy; I am not. Confession is necessary because this holds true. But what do we confess? And how? In the context of desire, we may want to begin by considering the tension of the Lord's Prayer—*Our Father* and *Your kingdom*—and identifying the imbalance of our desires. We sin by wanting too much from God. We also sin by wanting too little.

> We sin by wanting too much from God. We also sin by wanting too little.

Our Father helps us summon the courage to want. It invites us to believe that God is kind and generous and that, like an innocent child to his father, we can boldly confide our needs to him, expecting him to answer, and answer generously. It is an invitation into trust. "What father among you, if his son asks for a fish, will instead of a fish give him a serpent; or if he asks for an egg, will give him a scorpion?" (Luke 11:11-12). Herein lies our courage, our freedom and our boldness to risk wanting from God.

To what may be our surprise, C. S. Lewis, in his book *The Weight of Glory*, says that our greatest problem isn't in wanting too much, but in wanting too little.

It would seem that Our Lord finds our desires not too strong, but too weak. We are half-hearted creatures, fooling about with drink and sex and ambition when infinite joy is offered us, like an ignorant child who wants to go on making mud pies in a slum because he cannot imagine what is meant by the offer of a holiday at the sea.

We are far too easily pleased.[10]

The failure to want may not be contentment at all. It may be cowardice. We could be profoundly afraid to place our bets on God. When this kind of fear takes up residence in our hearts, we confess: Father, I have failed to fully trust your goodness.

Our desires for God's goodness, however, are chastened by the next phrase: *Your kingdom*. Through Jesus Christ, God purposes to return shalom to the earth. Jesus said,

> The Spirit of the Lord is upon me,
> because he has anointed me
> to proclaim good news to the poor.
> He has sent me to proclaim liberty to the captives
> and recovering of sight to the blind,
> to set at liberty those who are oppressed,
> to proclaim the year of the Lord's favor. (Luke 4:18-19)

God wills to undo oppression and to re-establish justice. But this is far too seldom the content of our prayers.

We do well to confess our consumerist impulses toward God. How often we come to him like an eager child comes to Santa, with a laundry list of self-serving requests rather than pleas to heal the world. In *Eat This Book*, Eugene Peterson notes the consumer approach we often take to the Bible. Consumers of the Bible hear what they want to hear and discard the rest—because consumers want satisfaction, 100-percent guaranteed. So long as God delivers on the bottom line, he keeps our business. But when he doesn't (arriving with a product we haven't ordered or according to a delivery schedule we haven't anticipated) we take our business elsewhere. Peterson cautions that we've supplanted the Trinity of Father, Son and Holy Spirit with a new trinity of "Holy

Needs, Holy Wants, and Holy Feelings. . . . The New Trinity doesn't get rid of God or the Bible, it merely puts them to the service of needs, wants and feelings."[11]

This is exactly the reflex Paul predicted in 2 Timothy 4:3-4: "For the time is coming when people will not endure sound teaching, but having itching ears they will accumulate for themselves teachers to suit their own passions, and will turn away from listening to the truth and wander off into myths." Consumerism leads to an ultimate rejection of God. We become like King Jehoiakim in Jeremiah 36, who hears the word of the Lord read aloud and, after every three or four columns, cuts the section off with a knife and throws it into the fire. The words of warning, which Jeremiah had recorded and God had meant for inspiring repentance, were disregarded. "Neither the king nor any of his servants who heard all these words was afraid, nor did they tear their garments" (Jeremiah 36:24). We must confess our eagerness for having our own way: Father, I have failed to love your Word and will.

There is no exhaustive checklist for confession. The Holy Spirit, speaking through the Holy Scriptures, can be relied on to help us understand when our desires point to a vision of flourishing in God—and when they do not. Our job is to remain open to the role of admitting. The illuminations we receive do not come as accusations. Rather, they arrive as invitations—to live more fully into the abundant life Jesus has promised (see John 10:10). Every occasion of conviction is God's gentle nudge into joy.

> We need not confess our desire for happiness, only confess when we have sought it in sources other than God.

Joy is central to John Piper's important book *Desiring God*. Piper calls himself a Christian hedonist who seeks his happiness in God. "The longing to be happy is a universal human experience, and it is good, not sinful," writes Piper. "We should never try to deny or resist our longing to be happy, as though it were a bad impulse. Instead, we should seek to intensify this longing and nourish it with whatever will provide the deepest and more enduring satisfaction . . . God."[12] Piper reminds us that we need not confess our desire for happiness, only confess when we have sought it in sources other than God.

❧

I call a friend to confess the ordinary tangles of an otherwise unextraordinary day. I blubber to this friend that I am meeting the ambiguities of our future with a desire to control. I am playing God again. I acknowledge the bitterness burrowing in my heart against Ryan for past sin and admit how stupidly good and powerful I feel to rehearse these sins, which should have long ago been forgiven and released. I then admit the continent I want to put between me and the emotionally needy people in my life, how I see them as drains on my nonrenewable resources, how I resent the imposition of their problems. I admit my love for all of these sins that bind. I confess that I cherish them and remain unwilling to walk in the freedom of obedience. I speak all this aloud to my friend because I desperately need to—because it makes my sin ugly. Desire requires these conversations. Desire requires these confessions. Desire will need to speak the truth if it is ever to own up to its nature.

She listens. She prays with me. I don't need her to tell me I'm okay, that sin is okay or that tomorrow will be better. I need her to give me the gospel, fully leaded, exploding with the power to re-create and renew and free, because no matter how hard I try, my heart is a desperate sieve. The good news leaks out.

Forgive us our sins.

We confess, agreeing with God on the brokenness and shame and suffering that sin visits upon us, others and, most of all, him. And then we allow Jesus to take it, to shoulder it, to bear it on our behalf. From there we travel light—and walk confidently into greater joy.

Reflection Questions

1. Consider the self you want to be and the self you are. What prevents you from owning these contradictions through the practice of confession?

2. If the sins of desire can be identified as either wanting too little from God or too much, of which are you most guilty?

3. Who in your life receives your regular confessions? Or whom might you want to invite into this role?

9

Be My Neighbor

Community

What a writer doesn't say is at least as interesting as what she does. For all of my confessional impulses and my writer-tell-all ethos, I have written very little about my marriage. What should be made of that silence? Does the ease with which, early into our marriage, I almost drove it against the rocks prove how extraordinarily tenuous our promise has been?

Ryan and I have been married seventeen years. Happily married. Marriage, for us, has motored along without giving us extraordinary trouble. We agree far more than we disagree and make the major and minor decisions families make—where to live, where to work, what priorities to cherish—without headaches. We enjoy one another's company, share our secrets and depend on each other for sanity. Ryan has successfully achieved what every husband might aspire to do: he has kept me laughing.

Our marriage is good. It is even enviable according to some who know us. But it is not a perfect marriage. No marriage is—although I may not be the one best suited for judging the measurable distance between good and near perfect in our case. Living inside a marriage prevents one from observing it accurately. It's akin to asking a fish how he likes his pond. Whether the water is murky or translucent, he doesn't know. It's water—and that's life to him.

Marriage, for me, is that pond. I don't ever want to live without it. But I can also admit to being conspicuously ungrateful for the marriage we have. In fact, were we to poll my husband, he would venture to say that I take him for granted. I know this because recently, when we were hugging before he left for a weekend away, he said to me matter-of-factly, "You take me for granted."

"You take *me* for granted," I insisted.

"I might not always show you the appreciation I feel," he defended, "but at least I feel it."

"So you're better because you feel it but don't say it?" I argued. "And I'm worse because I don't feel it?"

Neither is a respectable position.

Marriage is an ecosystem, a community. In marriage, there is the husband, the wife and the marriage itself, and the three-in-one trinity of marriage suffers neglect if left unattended. Perhaps neglect has been our greatest struggle in marriage. Ryan and I fail to regularly remind ourselves that every marriage—even good, reliable ones—need tending. We're busy and preoccupied people who value productivity and efficiency. We could be called ambitious. Busyness dawned long before the era of children, and our too-much-to-do hurry has had us perennially missing each other for most of our married life. I sometimes wonder what it will be like to grow old together: will we be able to slow gracefully like the elderly couples I sometimes see strolling hand-in-hand in the middle of the day down our neighborhood streets? I envy the hurry they have contentedly left behind. Will we also be able to leave the hurry behind?

There is no particular crisis that we face now in our marriage—only the crisis of life with its evolutionary change. The children grow, we grow and the marriage grows, and all this necessarily demands something more than static habits and hopes. We've got to continue working at this thing called marriage. No matter the condition of the water, we're fitted with gills, and water is the air we've got to keep breathing.

The eleven years that I was home with young children are just recently—and gratefully, I might add—put behind us. I don't mean to sound ungrateful for the tremendous privilege it has been to be the primary caregiver of our children. But it is also true that whenever I see a pregnant woman with a baby on her hip and a diaper bag slung over her shoulder (and other children clinging to any remaining available appendage), I heave a sigh of relief. Some days, there is no greater joy than going grocery shopping alone.

The years I was home manning the domestic front were the same years I released my husband into pursuing his career opportunities. Eight years he studied for actuarial exams, three years he worked to complete his MBA; he wanted to achieve these goals, and I helped him, if reluctantly at times. I was not always as willing a partner as I might have liked. For example, when he finished his exams and admitted he was thinking of pursuing an MBA, I emphatically said, "Absolutely not!"

Months later, in Sunday worship, God spoke into that place of resistance. *Would you really hold Ryan back from something I've called him to?*

Eventually, the intensity of childrearing in its early years and of Ryan's career demands yielded to a season of more time and flexibility for me. I started to want for things outside the home, and I found a home for those desires: I wrote. But in this process, which I'm just beginning, I'm discovering how I need my husband's essential partnership in the pursuit of those personal desires, just as he has needed mine. I need his affirmation, his encouragement. I need him to release me into this calling. Maybe I need it most because I'm so afraid that it's terribly selfish of me to hole up in our home office and pound out words on this page, neglecting the laundry for the second week in a row.

Letting marriage become this kind of exchange, where we negotiate our individual desires as well as the desires for our family, has been an arduous learning process for us, especially since it has upset, at least most recently, the apple cart of our domestic arrangement. Now that I am writing, even speaking, I have needed to ask for more help around the house. When there are retreats and conferences scheduled, sometimes I need Ryan home from work early to pick up the kids from school or dinner from Costco. There is difficulty in making this transition—for both of us. Yet in all the turbulence of turning over this domestic soil, I am unearthing something good and holy, even in the process of wanting and willing to write.

I've found a growing desire to make something beautiful of this arrangement we call marriage. I now more readily want the "I do's" to become the "I will's," and I wish them to finally resolve into the "I have's."

Let marriage be something I live well.

Community as Restraint

We're divorcing more readily than the generations before us. And just as marriage is suffering in modern times, human community as a whole is suffering. For as quickly and as easily as we can dissolve our marriages, we can choose to withdraw from our human communities.

If we don't like our neighborhood, we can move to a new one. If our church ceases to please us, we can shop for a better one. If our colleagues annoy us, we can always look for a new job with a better company. If our adult children disappoint us (or we them), contact can be severed. The transience of human society today allows everyone to maintain only the relationships they choose. Every human connection is a fragile thread and can be snipped at will.

> *Every human connection is a fragile thread and can be snipped at will.*

This ability to discard human relationships like last season's fashion makes us value our relationships too little. We haven't learned to work at them, only to discard them when they don't work. In his book *The Meaning of Marriage*, Tim Keller says our autonomy is owed to a new modern hierarchy of values. "After all, our culture makes individual freedom, autonomy, and fulfillment the very highest values, and thoughtful people know deep down that any love relationship at all means the loss of all three."[1]

Women, especially, are apt to see marriage and family as possible restraints on professional ambition, thereby making these things less undesirable. We are marrying later and having children later in order to more firmly establish ourselves in our careers. Publicly, the conversation drives toward figuring out how women can still have it "all" if or when they should choose to become a wife and mother. We can't stomach the idea of having to give something up.

The "all" women are chasing is an elusive ideal. When we belong to human community (marriage and family, as examples), it necessitates that we surrender some of our freedoms. Wendell Berry writes powerfully on the subject of community in his essay "Sex, Economy, Freedom and Community." He underlines the fact that the freedom of an individual is often opposed to the freedom of the community. Another way of saying this is that the *desire* of the individual is often opposed to the *desire* of the community.

> The individual, unlike the household and the community, always has two ways to turn: she or he may turn either toward the household and the community, to receive membership and to give service, or toward the relatively unconditional life of the public, in which one is free to pursue self-realization, self-aggrandizement, self-interest, self-fulfillment, self-enrichment, self-promotion, and so on. . . . The individual life implies no standard of behavior and responsibility.[2]

Berry is saying that if you have only yourself to think about, you are quite free to pursue your desires without restraint. If, however, you belong to a community (marriage, friendship, family, church), you must consider the impact of your desires and pursuits on those relationships. You must even revise them if the good of the community demands it.

Community then becomes its own kind of restraint on desire. This doesn't mean it is ugly or to be despised. On the contrary, community (and the restraints of our relationships) moderates selfishness; it even has the capacity for producing virtue. "Marriage, family life, friendship, neighborhood, and other personal connections . . . depend also on trust, patience, respect, mutual help, forgiveness—in other words, the *practice* of love, as opposed to the mere *feeling* of love."[3]

When we belong to community, in any and all of its various forms, we are forced to submit ourselves to the rigorous practice of love. As the apostle Paul describes in 1 Corinthians 13, love is an apprenticeship in patience, charity, generosity of goodwill, forgiveness and resilience. Love is the most perfect form of godly motivation: without it, we are nothing and gain nothing. To leave behind the childishness of self-absorption, we must mature into love.

> When we belong to community, we are forced to submit ourselves to the rigorous practice of love.

But, in order to love, we must also belong.

Life's Long View

Recently reading a book on time management (productivity, a-hem), I was struck by one man's view of time. In her book *Good Busy*, Julia Scatliff O'Grady interviewed ten different people for their perspective on time. Each chapter is titled metaphorically ("Buffer," "Tunnel," "Sliver," "Milk") to capture how that particular person views his or her time. Alexander X. Byrd, associate professor of history at Rice University, views his time *geologically*. Although his professional demands of research and publication and teaching are overwhelming, he resists the notion that speed is the key to success. Byrd doesn't give in to the pressures of hurry and worry. Instead, he keeps a long view on life. "What matters is the whole span of your life, not the one or two things you do or don't do now." What are his life goals? "See my children go to elementary school, die married, and go to heaven."[4]

Somehow that feels deeply biblical to me—considering our time geologically. It's the sanity of saying that we aren't as important as we think, that our lives are a wisp in the winds that bluster their way toward eternity, that we will be measured not by the incremental use of our minutes but by the architecture of our years.

Geological time helps the big things recover their proportion (for example, marriage). It also allows the little things to shrink to their proper stature. Recovering this geological vision—the scope of the temporal importance of our lives (not too big, not too small) against the kingdom of God (eternal, glorious and never-ending)—is important for desire. It carves a path to the first things.

The author of the book of Ecclesiastes is fascinated by the subjects of both time and desire. Written by the wisest of all men, King Solomon, at what may have been the end of his life, the book sounds the melancholy refrain of the passing of time.

> Vanity of vanities, says the Preacher,
>   vanity of vanities! All is vanity.
> What does man gain by all the toil
>   at which he toils under the sun?
> A generation goes, and a generation comes,
>   but the earth remains forever. (Ecclesiastes 1:2-4)

The king is disenchanted with work and pleasure, with wealth and honor. What good is life's accumulation when death means to destroy it, when desire itself fails?

Resigned to the process of aging, King Solomon begins to see the end—and thereby more rightly define the beginning. "Man is going to his eternal home," he says (Ecclesiastes 12:5). He reasons that the measure of a "successful" life by human standards of achievement hasn't always been accurate. "I saw that under the sun the race is not to the swift, nor the battle to the strong, nor bread to the wise, nor riches to the intelligent, nor favor to those with knowledge, but time and chance happen to them all. For man does not know his time" (Ecclesiastes 9:11-12). Those who live best live most conscious of geological time.

> Those who live best live most conscious of geological time.

When man doesn't know his time, when woman forgets her place in the grand galaxy of chronos, we forget the fundamental rules by which we are meant to live: "The end of the matter; all has been heard. Fear God and keep his commandments, for this is the whole duty of man. For God will bring every deed into judgment, with every secret thing, whether good or evil" (Ecclesiastes 12:13-14). Sinful desire substitutes small for big, temporal for eternal, and makes us lose our place in this big, spinning sphere.

Keep the commands.

Keep the "I do's" too.

(Non)Negotiable of Human Community

It would indeed be impossible to read the Bible without recognizing that godliness is formed in community. At least this is what God intends. The spiritual life is no maverick adventure. We aren't lone rangers. We belong to the plural people of God.

In the Old Testament, God calls a nation to be his people. Abraham is their father, and when Abraham's family grows beyond the capacity for being counted, they become a terror to the nation of Egypt, who fear their burgeoning strength. "Behold, the people of Israel are too many and too mighty for us. Come, let us deal shrewdly with them, lest they multiply, and, if war breaks out, they join our enemies and fight against us and escape from the land" (Exodus 1:9-10).

The Israelite slaves gain freedom from their Egyptian task-masters and, led by Moses, are taught to understand their identity as God's people. "Now therefore, if you will indeed obey my voice and keep my covenant, you shall be my treasured possession among all peoples, for all the earth is mine; and you shall be to me a kingdom of priests and a holy nation. These are the words that you shall speak to the people of Israel" (Exodus 19:5-6). This is no language of individualism. There is no private notion of following God. Everything for the ancient Israelites is team and togetherness, for better or for worse. (And worse it is, as the first generation of the exodus fails to trust God and is cursed to wander in the wilderness until death.)

In the New Testament, the people of God are called the people of God not because of ethnic identity—"There is neither Jew nor Greek"—but because of their identity found in Jesus Christ. The *ekklesia*, or "called out" ones, is the church.

> You are a chosen race, a royal priesthood, a holy nation, a people for his own possession, that you may proclaim the excellencies of him who called you out of darkness into his marvelous light. Once you were not a people, but now you are God's people; one you had not received mercy, but now you have received mercy. (1 Peter 2:9-10)

Peter obviously borrows language from Exodus, and the implication is the same. God isn't calling individual persons to follow his Son Jesus: he is seeking to "purify for himself a people [plural] for his own possession who are zealous for good works" (Titus 2:14). We surrender to Jesus—and necessarily join the church.

At the end of the Bible, in the book of Revelation, heaven is pictured as a city: "Behold, the dwelling place of God is with man. He will dwell with them, and they will be his people, and God himself will be with them as their God. He will wipe away every tear from their eyes, and death shall be no more" (Revelation 21:3-4). A city is a place of corporate belonging. Heaven is the eternal city where we, all together, like a bride, finally and fully belong to our husband, Jesus.

If these examples to say that our identity in Christ is a corporate one aren't obvious enough, consider the incarnation. When God chose to reveal the fullness of his being to humanity, he chose the vehicle of the body and the medium of human relationship. For thirty-three years, Jesus lived as a man. He was born into a family. He had a mother, brothers and sisters, and he hailed from a small village—albeit not a spectacularly significant one (see John 1:46). God doesn't despise these human connections of community; through the incarnation, he elevates their status by saying that this is precisely where he is at work: at the anvil of life upon life.

Self-Made Loneliness

Modern society is losing its appetite for community. David Brooks, a columnist for *The New York Times*, has been sounding the alarm regarding our growing bent toward individualism. In his essay "What Our Words Tell Us," Brooks points out how our language is even trending toward individualism. A recent study, which mined Google's database of all books published between 1500 and 2008, found that communal phrases are disappearing in favor of individual ones. *Personalized, self, standout, unique* and *I come first* are relatively new phrases to the modern lexicon. They are being substituted for words that point to a more corporate view of identity (*collective, common good, tribe, share, united* and *band together*).

In another column, "The Talent Society," Brooks notes that "fifty years ago, America was groupy. People were more likely to be enmeshed in stable, dense and obligatory relationships. They were more defined by permanent social roles: mother, father, deacon. Today, individuals have more freedom. They move between more diverse, loosely structured and flexible networks of relationships."

Brooks has noted that the more individualistic we become, the greater we prize our freedoms and the more we despise our restraints. "People no longer even have a language to explain why freedom should sometimes be limited. The results are as predicted.

A decaying social fabric, especially among the less fortunate. Decline in marriage. More children raised in unsteady homes. Higher debt levels as people spend to satisfy their cravings."[5] Our freedom, as Brooks puts it, is buying our cultural demise because we're using our freedoms to break the bonds of community, which have long held us together.

In a provocative article appearing in *The Atlantic*, Stephen Marche makes the argument that technology is destroying community. He opens the article at the scene of Yvette Vickers's death. The former Playboy playmate and actress was found dead in her home after a period of many months. The death of the eighty-three-year-old woman had gone unnoticed until a neighbor finally recognized that Vickers's mail had long been accumulating. This neighbor, searching for clues to understand her anonymous neighbor, searched Vickers's phone bills for answers. What she found were calls made to distant fans (whose acquaintance she had made from the Internet), but no contact or connection with family or friends.

Marche observes that "Vickers's web of connections had grown broader but shallower, as has happened for many of us."[6] He notes how "we live in an accelerating contradiction: the more connected we become, the lonelier we are. We were promised a global village; instead we inhabit the drab cul-de-sacs and endless freeways of a vast suburb of information."[7] He concludes that social media, despite all its promise of connection and community, actually isolates us.

We are hardwired for relationship. Biblically, this is true because we are made in the image of a relational God. "It is not good for man to be alone," God declared when he surveyed his creation in Genesis 2. He made a helper and companion for Adam, someone better suited with whom to share his life than, say, the zebras and wild boar.

Sociological research is confirming what the Bible has been saying forever. Loneliness may be more pronounced in the preoccupied era of the smartphone, but we've always craved human connection. This would seem an opportune time for the local church to ride a white horse of rescue into the barren wilderness of anonymity. After all, community is supposed to be our gig. Unfortunately, people aren't turning to the church for solace from loneliness. They may actually be running away from it in droves.

In a three-year research study, the Barna Group set out to examine perceptions "outsiders" have of the evangelical church. They sampled sixteen- to twenty-nine-year-olds and found that less than 20 percent of them could agree to this statement: "Christian churches accept and love people unconditionally, regardless of how people look or what they do." Even more troubling was that less than half of "insiders" (those who actually attend church) could agree either.

What words did outsiders use to characterize evangelical churches and born-again Christians? *Hypocritical. Judgmental.* Outsiders admit they perceive Christians as unwilling to listen and consider the opinions of others. "What they react negatively to is our 'swagger,' how we go about things and the sense of self-importance we project," writes Kinnaman, who published Barna's research in his book *unChristian.* He claims outsiders consider us intolerant, bigoted and sheltered, and this repels what might otherwise have been their genuine interest in Christianity. "Sometimes young outsiders venture into churches, and often they come with an intense load of difficult experiences and deep hurts. They do not want to be scolded; they require our help and empathy."[8]

Church should be an antidote for human loneliness. Church should be the place to find belonging and acceptance. But sometimes, it wounds more than it heals.

It Was the Best of Church, It Was the Worst of Church

I spent several years in recovery, rehabilitating from the church, licking the wounds I suffered there. I don't necessarily want to detail what happened, primarily because I don't intend to reopen what has since healed. I can say, with profound gratitude, that by God's great mercy, the pastors and lay leaders at all of the various churches we've attended over the years have been well intentioned; their desire has been to serve Christ and his church faithfully. Nonetheless, they have been imperfect people—and imperfect people get it wrong sometimes. When they do, their unforced errors threaten the trust we place in church.

Though my husband and I had our own ways of dealing with the silent outrage when the church wounded us deeply, we never actually stopped going to church. I suppose you could say that we nudged ourselves to heal in the *idea* of church if not in the *reality* of it. Prodded by the Scriptures, we hoped beyond hoping that we were made for the church and the church for us, and we could see no other way forward than to persist in the practice of *as we forgive*.

The Lord's Prayer anchors us in the moments where the church wounds. It will not let us forget that we are made for community, that like it or not, we had better

> The Lord's Prayer anchors us in the moments where the church wounds.

learn to get along. This prayer is a prayer for the church. It is a plural prayer. It is a song to be sung in chorus. Give *us* this day *our* daily bread, forgive *us* our sins as *we* forgive those who have sinned against *us*: every assumption is communal rather than individual. The Lord's Prayer doesn't tolerate Horatio Alger myths of self-sovereignty, self-reliance, self-love. Just by nature of its communal posture, the Lord's Prayer forces us back into the fabric of our human relationships and obligates us to parents, to spouses, to friends—most of all, to the church.

The Lord's Prayer has been our guide throughout this book: it commends to us ways for discerning our desires. It envisions our freedoms as well as recognizes our constraints. The prayer, at least for me, has served as a theological fence: its language corrals my wild horses of desire and restricts me from wandering off into dangerous woods. I find safety in the refuge of these words. But restriction is not the only purpose of a fence: it also encloses pasture. "The lines have fallen for me in pleasant places; indeed, I have a beautiful inheritance" (Psalm 16:6). The Lord's Prayer leads us to the spaciousness of God's good—even the good of church.

Pilgrim Friendships

We need church. But we don't need it like medicine. We don't swallow it down for good health, and we don't grin and bear our togetherness—although, in the wake of grievance, I understand how it can feel like that. In spite of our experiences of the church's betrayal this side of heaven, the Bible insists church is meant for our good.

When I say church (or biblical community), for my purposes here, I mean the local congregation of believers. Certainly that is not the only biblical meaning of the word. Church, as the Bible uses the word, is both universal and local. However, it is always assumed in the Scriptures that a believer belongs to both.

"A local or individual church," writes Thomas Oden, "is a company of those who are united in any given place in faith in Jesus Christ for worship, proclamation, and service in Christ."[9] Local church, as *place* and *company,* implies that people must be physically present in order to belong.

We aren't part of the local church in any meaningful way if our name only figures on a membership roll and we deliberately choose not to participate in its gatherings. We aren't part of the church if, sitting in our living rooms in Omaha, we're tuning in to a podcast of a local church in LA. We're part of a church (local) when we've lost some of our anonymity and begin to know and be known. And by that definition, local church is the generous invitation to belong. It's an antidote for alienation, isolation and the unbearable loneliness of believing no one knows us or cares to. We're closer to understanding God's unconditional love for us as we find it in the company of God's people.

The church is the place where we are meant to receive the encouragement and help we need as we journey toward holiness. Every pilgrim needs a friend. And we need friends who will tell us the truth, incapable as we are of seeing it for ourselves. It matters in this whole business of desire if we're going solo or traveling in a pack. Because the church is a truth-telling community.

In the book of Galatians, Paul teaches about the responsibility we bear for one another's spiritual health and well-being. "If anyone is caught in any transgression, you who are spiritual should restore him in a spirit of gentleness" (6:1). We cannot remain indifferent to one another. We can't stand at the sidelines while our friends in Christ have been tackled by temptation, when they've been concussed by sin.

We owe it to one another—let's call it duty—to stand guard over each other and keep watch, to flag when a situation seems perilous and someone is in spiritual danger. "Bear one another's burdens, and so fulfill the law of Christ," Paul implores, begging the church of Galatia (and us) to remember that allegiance to Christ means loyalty to his people (6:2). The church is a body: "If one member suffers, all suffer together; if one member is honored, all rejoice together" (1 Corinthians 12:26). The church is composed of interdependent parts: hands need feet like elbows need eyes. A solitary Christian who thinks he can live independently of the church functions about as well as a thumb severed from its hand.

As much as I might sometimes wish that my experience of church were better and closer to the biblical ideal, I could not have lived without the imperfect church I have had. I have told my own story of potentially catastrophic temptation in chapter three, but what I failed to mention was the friend who mitigated the would-be disaster. She and I had been in a church small group together for several years and found a spiritual friendship and accountability that seemed comfortable and easy. But I never told her about the flirtation I was enjoying at work—at least not until I had told Ryan.

Admitting to him what had happened allowed me to eventually also admit it to her. I wanted her to know, sensing instinctively that when she did, I would hem myself into another layer of safety.

One night over coffee, I told her everything that had been happening at work, and she listened patiently and graciously. Then she spun me her own woeful tale of infidelity. She and her fiancé had been separated during their engagement while he was finishing a graduate degree. During that year of separation, she grew steadily attracted to a colleague at work. They flirted. Soon enough, she was spending nights at his apartment, always waking up the next morning to the resolve that it would never happen again. But it did. The horrors of that treachery grew like gangrene. She was sickened by the deception, but the secrecy gave it shelf life.

Eventually, she broke off that relationship and told her fiancé. He forgave her, and they married—but their marriage has suffered the ill effects of the deception and the betrayal. Forgive and forget aren't always so easily paired.

Don't do that, she begs me. *It's not worth it.*

I already knew this to be true—that my marriage was worth infinitely more than a momentary flirtation, however innocent that may once have seemed. But I needed her to tell me. In fact, as she told me, it became *more* true than it had previously been. This is the channeled power of community.

In community, we bear the Word of Christ to one another, and the Word gains volume and clarity. It speaks louder and with more force than when it reverberates inside our own heads. "Let the Word of Christ dwell in you richly, teaching and admonishing one another in all wisdom, singing psalms and hymns and spiritual songs, with thankfulness in your hearts to God" admonishes the apostle Paul (Colossians 3:16).

What I've described in the story of my friend is not church per se, but an extension of church. In church, we commit to the worship of Christ and gather under the authority of God's Word. We submit ourselves together to our Lord, remembering with gratitude the broken body and blood and endeavoring to live faithfully to the commission he has left with us to go and make disciples (Matthew 28:19-20). We worship together as the church—the gathered people of God—and there we change.

The church is the best place to form the habits that shape our desires. In fact, as James K. A. Smith argues in *Desiring the Kingdom*, apart

> *The church is the best place to form the habits that shape our desires.*

from the church, there are no meaningful spiritual practices. "There are no 'private' practices. . . . There are no practices without institutions."[10] In regard to the specific practice of reading and interpreting Scripture, Smith says, "The letters and documents that came to be the New Testament . . . functioned primarily in a liturgical context of worship, not the private context of individual study."[11] Coming together to submit ourselves to God and to sound in unison our willingness to obey Christ drives those holy desires deeper. There is a mysterious, unparalleled holy energy when believers gather together for church.

Lesson from History

Dietrich Bonhoeffer, a German pastor who was eventually executed by the Nazis on April 8, 1945, wrote convincingly on the subject of Christian community in his book *Life Together*. He wrote about the "inexhaustible . . . riches that open up for those who by God's will are privileged to live in the daily fellowship of life with other Christians," a privilege he invariably enjoyed during his days as leader of a seminary for the German Confessing Church.[12] The seminary functioned like a small monastic community where the Word of God was not simply imbibed; it was lived. *Practiced.*

This community of seminarians became an essential anchor for Bonhoeffer as he struggled to reconcile his obligations to his country with his loyalty to Christ and suffered the splintering of his conscience. "It is remarkable how I am never quite clear about the motives for any of my decisions. Is that a sign of confusion, or inner dishonesty, or is it a sign that we are guided without our knowing, or is it both? . . . In the last resort one acts from a level which remains hidden to us."[13]

In those agonizing moments of self-doubt, Bonhoeffer looked to other believers to be reminded of the righteousness he could find through Jesus Christ. "The Christian needs another Christian who speaks God's Word to him," wrote Bonhoeffer.[14] "He knows that God's Word in Jesus Christ pronounces him guilty, even when he does not feel his guilt, and God's Word in Jesus Christ pronounces him not guilty and righteous, even when he does not feel that he is righteous at all."[15] The Word of God—proclaimed in and through and among the church—moors us to reality, the reality that no matter the true nature of our desires and thoughts, our actions and intentions, our righteousness is secure in Christ.

In the months leading up to his death, Bonhoeffer understood the enormous privilege of Christian community. In prison, he was relegated to letters and occasional visits from his Christian brothers and sisters. No longer could he enjoy the daily fellowship he had once known at the seminary.

> It is true, of course, that what is an unspeakable gift of God for the lonely individual is easily disregarded and trodden under foot by those who have the gift every day. It is easily forgotten that the fellowship of Christian brethren is a gift of grace, a gift of the Kingdom of God that any day may be taken from us, that the time that still separates us from utter loneliness may be brief indeed. Therefore, let him who until now has had the privilege of living a common Christian life with other Christians praise God's grace from the bottom of his heart.[16]

The church is no perfect place, and we are not perfect people. But its deficiencies and ours invite us into the regular, rhythmic practice of grace, exactly where it is needed most: at the point of human connection. As the church, we can and should become the community where love and truth abide the complicated journey toward holiness. The church can learn how to speak and keep silent, how to bear the Word of God and the human story. We are, after all, the body of Jesus Christ.

Worship Local

Our senior pastor finds me after the service has concluded. "Can I borrow your wife for a second?" he asks Ryan, not waiting for an answer before grabbing me by the elbow and leading me out of the crowded hallway.

> *As the church, we can and should become the community where love and truth abide the complicated journey toward holiness.*

"We want you to lead the children's ministry," my pastor says without preamble. "I know you've just finished your book, and you don't have a lot of time. But give us ten or fifteen hours a week," he pleads, assuming, for the next five minutes, permission to reason why I am the person best suited for the job. Learning this has something to do with grey hair and the gaggle of kids following me into church every Sunday, I feel in no way extraordinarily flattered.

I steel myself with a thousand nos. I love children (particularly my own), but I know the administrative and thankless nature of children's ministry. Children's ministry is a ministry that everyone wants done well—and no one wants to do. Moreover, shouldering the responsibilities for children's ministry in a young and growing church like ours (where babies are multiplying like dandelions in a patch of grass) is not a hassle I fancy, not when my life is already crowded with family demands and writing.

"I'll think about it," I say. But I don't honestly give it careful consideration until the following Tuesday, when I'm in the church office hunting down books to complete the footnoting for this book.

"Kim and I are praying you'll take the job," our associate pastor says, explaining the extraordinary stress the ministry had produced in recent months for him and the elders.

I don't really want the job. I know my life will be easier without it. But I decide, by the end of the week, to take it. And I do so willingly.

I don't take the job, as I might have in years past, because I'm convinced that its difficulties ensure its virtue. I take it because I strongly believe that holy desire is cultivated in and for the local church. God means for us to belong to human community. In order for desire to be protected from its journey east, we will need to humble ourselves and implicate ourselves in the ordinary, honest and usually messy endeavors of the local church, praying for the grace to survive the ways we fail it and the ways it fails us. And for the occasions of disappointment, even grief, we will seize upon the privilege of praying as our Lord taught us to pray:

Forgive us our sins, as we forgive those who sin against us.

Reflection Questions

1. What inspires your love for Jesus' church? Your loathing?

2. If you began praying for the desire to belong more fully not only to God but to God's people, what would you hope to change?

3. What desires must you now set aside for the good of your communities (marriage, family, friendship, neighborhood, church, workplace)? To what extent do you do this willingly?

10

Ruby Slippers

Commitment

For millennia, we've been passing down our stories, holding fast to the idea that the conservation of story is the preservation of people. A story has the capacity for making us human. And the Bible tells the best stories, especially the story of the incarnate God-Man who pitched his tent among his people, making the lame to walk and the blind to see. He forgave sins. The story too big to be contained by all the libraries of the world is the story that has captured me (see John 21:25).

The Bible begins with stories in a vastly different time and place than our own. We easily come to them with hesitance, wondering if they can speak into our lives with relevance and with power. Yet I think we are surprised how quickly we locate ourselves in the threads of their narratives and names.

"These are the generations of the heavens and the earth" (Genesis 2:4).

"This is the book of the generations of Adam" (Genesis 5:1).

"These are the generations of Noah" (Genesis 6:9).

"These are the generations of Terah" (Genesis 11:27).

"These are the generations of Ishmael" (Genesis 25:12).

"These are the generations of Isaac" (Genesis 25:19).

"These are the generations of Esau" (Genesis 36:1).

"These are the names of the descendants of Israel" (Genesis 46:8).

We find ourselves in these stories, even in the story of the incarnate God-Man, and discover it to be perplexingly true that God has woven holiness into the human story. Why should he choose human frailty as a medium for his artistry? I'm not sure that I know, but the refrain from Genesis—*these are the generations*—affirms that God has dignified men and women and their stories. *These are the generations* helps me trust my desire, even my ambition, to write. I will keep at keeping my story because God is to be found here—in this record.

The names of men and women figure importantly in Genesis; so do the names of God. In one particular story, a woman even dares to name God.

"Hagar, where have you come from and where are you going?" asks the angel when he finds Hagar by a spring of water. Sarah has sent her servant away after she has conceived a child with Abraham, her husband. Hagar recounts this bitter disappointment to the angel, who then instructs her to return to Sarah. First, however, Hagar is promised a son—and this unexpected turn of grace makes Hagar lion-hearted. Hagar names *God*.

"You are a God of seeing" (Genesis 16:13).

In John's Gospel, we read of Mary Magdalene's encounter with the resurrected Jesus. When Mary Magdalene hurries to Jesus' tomb after a sabbath of darkness, she finds the stone rolled away and the tomb empty. In her blinding grief and confusion, she fails to recognize the man who approaches and calls her woman.

"Why are you weeping? Whom are you seeking?" Jesus asks (John 20:15).

But Mary, mistaking Jesus for the gardener, asks him to take her to the body of her crucified Lord, insisting that she can assume responsibility for it.

"Mary."

The irony may well be that when we fail to recognize Jesus, either because we are disoriented by grief, blinded by sin or even inoculated by simple disinterest, the first name and face we have capacity for recognizing is our own.

"Saul, Saul, why are you persecuting me?" (Acts 9:4).

Jen.

God is protagonist in each of our stories. Borrowing a phrase from Greek poetry, Paul made this very point standing in the middle of the Areopagus: "In him we live and move and have our being" (Acts 17:26-28). Every human story, having been scripted by God, has revelatory power. *Keep your story* was God's command to the Israelites. *Tell it to your children and your grandchildren,* "so that they should set their hope in God and not forget the works of God, but keep his commandments" (Psalm 78:7). *Rehearse the details of my salvation and deliverance so that you will not forget, so that you will remember to obey.* Storytelling and story keeping: these are holy acts of faith. They preserve faithfulness.

When Paul wrote his first letter to the church in Thessalonica, he explicitly names his missionary strategy while living among them and proclaiming the gospel to them: "We were ready to share

> *Storytelling and story keeping: these are holy acts of faith. They preserve faithfulness.*

with you not only the gospel of God but also our own selves, because you had become very dear to us" (1 Thessalonians 2:8). We shared with you our stories, Paul said. Now remember them—as good news.

These are the generations.

I take courage from the biblical record of story because it's my own story I have told in the pages of this book. I haven't shared it because it has been inimitably virtuous but because desire takes shape in the particularities of our lives. We cannot excerpt desire from the anthology of our stories. Our desires say something about us—who we have been, who we are and who we are becoming. They tell a part of the story that God is telling through us, even the beautiful and complicated story of being human and becoming holy.

These are the generations.

Genesis is a book of beginnings and blessings. And if it is a book about unfaithful starts—Adam—it is also a book about faithful endings—Abraham. I trust, by grace, that my story will, at the end of my days, have traveled that distance.

Loss: Revision of Desire

I have needed, in this book, to make a return to my own stories of loss. This has surprised me. Last July, I decided to call Kent State University and get my hands on a copy of my father's dissertation. He had finished a PhD in communications at Kent State when I was in elementary school, and some of the earliest memories I have of him are of his head bent over a typewriter in the basement bedroom of our Tennessee home. My brother and I did not have strict instructions to leave him alone, but I don't ever remember entering the bedroom while he was typing furiously at those electric keys.

What was the topic of his dissertation? In the middle of summer, in the middle of Toronto, at the age of thirty-eight, no external force had acted upon me to recall the phantom of my father's memory. It had been more than twenty years since a stranger found me in that crowded college cafeteria to tell me that my father was dead. But suddenly, I was thinking of his dissertation, on a July morning with our swimming suits and sand buckets stowed in the trunk of our car. What had transported me there?

Story.

To fill the blank pages of story, one must recover fossils of the past. Writing has been for me this archaeological dig, and I have retrieved my artifacts. Miles away from the site of excavation, I dig up memories and turn over sadness. The acute grief I presently feel for events that have happened long ago catches me, still now, unaware, and in the past two years, I have cried more than in the previous ten years. Tending to desire (and all matters of the heart) will have this unintended effect: waking from our numb state, we will begin to feel again.

I had not planned to tell the stories of the deaths of my father and brother, but pain has been like a centripetal force, forcing me back to the center of reality. If I thought I had buried those stories long ago with the bodies of the father and the brother that I lost as a young woman, they are now exhumed. But maybe those losses are the most credible stories I have to tell. And maybe it's been necessary to clear the path of desire from its typical debris.

Desire must surrender its clammy will to script its own endings and have its own way— that is, if it wants to continue calling itself a partner to faith. Maybe this is why loss is so necessary to holy desire and why "suffering produces endurance, and endurance produces character, and character produces hope" (Romans 5:3-4). Perhaps we should not be surprised that our losses are to be counted as joy, "for you know that the testing of your faith produces steadfastness. And let steadfastness have its full effect, that you may be perfect and complete, lacking in nothing" (James 1:3-4). Our losses mature us into the knowledge that we cannot play God, and we will need to remember this if we are to hold in proper tension the nature of holy desire, which is both the will to want and the willingness to surrender.

When Peter met the resurrected Jesus on the shore of the Sea of Tiberias, it was after a long night of unsuccessful fishing. As day

Desire must surrender its clammy will to script its own endings and have its own way—that is, if it wants to continue calling itself a partner to faith.

dawned, Jesus beckoned the sailors to "cast the net on the right side of the boat, and you will find some [fish]" (John 21:6). They had a miraculous catch, and Jesus fried up breakfast. When the disciples finished eating, Jesus asked Peter the same question three times: "Do you love me?" "Yes, I love you," came Peter's reply each time. But at the third go-round of the test of allegiance, Peter began showing exasperation. "Lord, you know everything; you know that I love you" (v. 17).

"Feed my sheep," Jesus said.

> "Truly, truly, I say to you, when you were young, you used to dress yourself and walk wherever you wanted, but when you are old, you will stretch out your hands, and another will dress you and carry you where you do not want to go." (This he said to show by what kind of death he was to glorify God.) And after saying this he said to him, "Follow me." (vv. 17-19)

Jesus insisted that faith would cost Peter his self-sovereignty. As Peter grew older, at least from an outsider's perspective, he would seem to be losing, rather than gaining his freedoms. The gospel would appear to be heading away from the direction of desire, even into the arms of death. But without apology, Jesus never retreated from the exacting demands of discipleship. He laid claim to control. "I will follow you wherever you go," one man panted as Jesus made his way for Jerusalem—and the cross. "Foxes have holes, and birds of the air have nests, but the Son of Man has nowhere to lay his head" (Luke 9:58). Another man promised to follow Jesus after he had buried his father. "Leave the dead to bury their own dead. But as for you, go and proclaim the kingdom of God" (v. 60). A third man asked to say his goodbyes to his family before following Jesus. "No one who puts his hand to the plow and looks back is fit for the kingdom of God" (v. 62). Never was Jesus afraid to insist on his own terms, even if it meant dissuading people from their intentions of faith and following.

Jesus upbraids our fanciful imaginings about the gospel's good news. With fierce regularity, Jesus upended the expectations of others like he overturned the temple tables of exchange. Crowds sought Jesus for their bread and for healing, and Jesus affirmed that whoever "feeds on my flesh and drinks my blood has eternal life" (John 6:56). Jesus scorned the piously religious; he embraced beggars and prostitutes instead. Jesus regaled crowds with stories of prodigals come home. He made heroes of Samaritans. Accused of being a drunkard and a glutton, Jesus was the conspicuous friend of tax collectors and sinners. "Zacchaeus, hurry and come down, for I must stay at your house today" (Luke 19:5). Jesus did not suffer human expectations for what the kingdom of God should be and achieve. He embraced a cross. The surprising nature of Jesus' life surprises our desires.

At every occasion, Jesus incarnated surprise: a baby born in a manger, a man crucified between two criminals. As God, he seemed to almost make

> The surprising nature of Jesus' life surprises our desires.

himself deliberately unrecognizable. "He was in the world, and the world was made through him, yet the world did not know him. He came to his own, and his own people did not receive him" (John 1:10-11). But there were those to whom was granted the faith to behold the glory of that mystery and to welcome it. This invitation is made to each of us today, not only to see Jesus as he really is but to surrender to the claims of discipleship as they really are. God may not give us the life we want or expect—and this can still be called good. He will force necessary revisions on our desires, especially through our experiences of disappointment and loss. This will seem painful. It will expose our myths of self-sovereignty. It will wrestle our will for control.

But it will also oblige us to trust—and trust welcomes us into a greater inheritance.

The Lord is my chosen portion and my cup;
　　you hold my lot.
The lines have fallen for me in pleasant places;
　　indeed, I have a beautiful inheritance . . .
You make known to me the path of life;
　　in your presence there is fullness of joy;
　　at your right hand are pleasures forevermore. (Psalm
　　　16:5-6, 11)

Limits—and Love

Despite my early occasions of loss—the death of my father at eighteen, the death of my brother at twenty-three—my myths of self-sovereignty have persisted with fierce intransigence. The habit of self-rule dies a slow and painful death. It has the devilish, indomitable will to survive.

> *The habit of self-rule dies a slow and painful death. It has the devilish, indomitable will to survive.*

Gratefully, mine yielded slightly more the day an ultrasound technician introduced me to Baby A and Baby B, and I called my husband to tell him the news.

"Is everything OK?" Ryan asked as soon as he picked up the phone.

"Everything's great," I reassured falsely, lingering over a dramatic pause. "We're having twins."

"Shut up!"

"No, I'm serious. We're having twins."

A long silence unwound. Finally, I heard him whisper.

Wow.

I understand the seismic surprise, indignation and even grief that seizes us when the future as we've planned and prepared for disintegrates. In theory, I might have been theologically committed to the idea that God had the right to order my life events. In reality, I was beholden to the notion that I was in control. My story is the struggle between the space of acknowledging God's sovereignty and calling it good. It is a story of laying down desire—and taking up surprise.

Several weeks ago, I stood watching Baby A and Baby B, now almost six years old, from the window of my bedroom. They were riding their bikes up and down the sidewalk in front of our house. Spring had been delinquent, but on this day, the sun had finally dawned glorious over Toronto and worked to thaw the lingering chill of winter.

I stared at them. Who was who? *Oh yeah, the red helmet. Colin wears the red helmet.* And of course—he would be the one wearing his rain boots under this first cloudless sky of April. Andrew was behind him, riding furiously to keep up with the brother who seemed to always outpace him. He was losing grip on his pedals at every other rotation. They were laughing together, and their bikes were an exuberant parade of fun.

Then, a collision.

Colin's bike turned over and dumped him sprawling on the sidewalk. He started crying. But before I could move from the window, Nathan, their older brother who had also been playing in the front yard, dropped his basketball and rushed to Colin's side. He murmured words of consolation in his little brother's ear, and Colin stopped crying. He brushed his knees, and with his brother's help, stood to his feet and mounted his bike again.

It has been six years since learning I was carrying twins. The aftershocks have quelled, and we are settled into the surprise. And, as time will do, it has given up some of its secrets. Why did I have to lay down a desire (for graduate school, for ministry) that seemed good? Why did I have to assume a life (a family) that seemed disproportionately bigger than my capacities? What had God purposed in this unexpected, even unwanted, detour?

I can't presume to fully understand God and his ways, but I think I can lay claim to this knowledge: life's impossibilities and the limits they force upon us are often where we grow most quickly in our desire for God. Before having five children, I had wanted to be present at every scene of collision. But when the twins were born and I needed help for the simplest tasks (grocery shopping, preschool carpooling), I started growing more fully into grace, the grace that is made available to us in our weaknesses and limitations. This grace was my only alternative. "My grace is sufficient for you, for my power is made perfect in weakness" (2 Corinthians 12:9). I brought home those two little bundles from the hospital and made a welcome return to the gospel: the good news that Jesus is sufficient when I am not.

> Life's impossibilities and the limits they force upon us are often where we grow most quickly in our desire for God.

Those early years of five children running amok became perhaps the most hopeful time of my life, even as they were the most difficult. I discovered a new freedom in admitting that I couldn't manage. I even discovered that God required so much less of me than the rigorous self-imposed burdens I had grown used to. I wasn't disciplined. I didn't rise early to read the Scriptures. The only spiritual effort I exerted during those first months was to copy Psalm 145 on lined index cards and tuck them into the pocket of the glider, pulling them out when I nursed the boys. I did little else than consider God's love for me and for our family. It renewed hope.

One doesn't have to be the mother of a large family to understand that the most difficult and demanding circumstances of our lives are God's wise prescription for discovering that his strength is greater than our own. We pray best when we need God most. "Dependency is the heartbeat of prayer," writes Paul Miller in *A Praying Life*.[1] "If you are not praying, then you are quietly confident that time, money, and talent are all you need in life. You'll always be a little too tired, a little too busy. But if, like Jesus, you realize you can't do life on your own, then no matter how busy, no matter how tired you are, you will find the time to pray."[2] We all have to find ourselves, at some point, stuck with a life that we have not wanted or that feels too difficult to bear, because this may be the most persuasive invitation we have to get on our knees—and thirst for God.

If motherhood has taught me about my greater need of God, it has also delivered me from the ambition to be spectacular for God. These years have worked steadily to erode some of my eastward pretensions of calling. "Beware of practicing your righteousness before other people in order to be seen by them," Jesus warned.

> *We pray best when we need God most.*

> When you give to the needy, sound no trumpet before you, as the hypocrites do in the synagogues and in the streets, that they may be praised by others. . . . But when you give to the needy, do not let your left hand know what your right hand is doing so that your giving may be in secret. And your Father who sees in secret will reward you. (Matthew 6:1-4)

Secrecy can deliver us from our proud ambitions. Invisibility can purify the offerings that we bring to God.

There is considerable secrecy in motherhood (and fatherhood, for that matter). No one stands to applaud when a mother patiently entreats the child who tries disappearing when it's his turn to clear the table. No one notices when she's deftly managed the unruly expectations of the final month of school. No one cheers when she is serving broccoli for dinner or packing carrots for lunch. A mother contents herself to do work that is small, invisible, unspectacular and often unappreciated. She may want to step beyond the mundane, but remaining is one way of learning holiness.

"We want life to have meaning, we want fulfillment, healing and even ecstasy, but the human paradox is that we find these things by starting where we are, not where we wish we were. We must look for blessings to come from unlikely, everyday places—out of Galilee, as it were—and not in spectacular events, such as the coming of a comet," writes Kathleen Norris in her essay "The Quotidian Mysteries."[3]

Holiness is formed in us more unspectacularly and more incrementally than we expect—wherever the practice of small, everyday faithfulness is required of us. Somewhere, somehow, God is asking each of us to do something so entirely common as to love someone. If we let the truth of this sit on our skin—that we are one in seven billion, a speck on the still point of the turning world, the present pinhead *I* in the enormous bulk of human history—it has potential for allowing us to be swept into the grand calling to be small, smaller, smallest for the kingdom. As John the Baptist said, servants don't fear their shrinking size. "He must increase, but I must decrease" (John 3:30). Praise the Father who, despite our clamoring desire for the limelight, gives instead obscurity and the obligation to love as a means for purifying our ambitions of calling.

> *Holiness is formed in us more unspectacularly and more incrementally than we expect—wherever the practice of small, everyday faithfulness is required of us.*

At Proper Speed

Loss and limits—though these have chastened my desires, they have not extinguished them. For how do we get on our knees and leave off desire? How do we pray without wanting? This is the tension I keep meeting in my own journey of faith: that the very kind of prayer that forces me to surrender is also the prayer that needles me to want. The Lord's Prayer is this kind of prayer, held together in the abiding belief that the Father who is in sovereign control of the world cares enough about me to solicit my request for bread.

In fact, the Bible invites each of us to prayerful acts of "impudence." When Jesus told a parable about prayer, he recounted the story of a man asleep at midnight who was awakened by the sound of his neighbor knocking at his door. The neighbor calls out, "Friend, lend me three loaves" (Luke 11:5). The neighbor had had a visit from an unexpected guest, and his cupboard was bare.

"Do not bother me," his friend answers. "The door is now shut, and my children are with me in bed. I cannot get up and give you anything" (v. 7). But the neighbor was not to be put off. He persisted in knocking, knocking more and more loudly.

> *The very kind of prayer that forces me to surrender is also the prayer that needles me to want.*

"I tell you," Jesus explains, "though he will not get up and give him anything because he is his friend, yet because of his *impudence* he will rise and give him whatever he needs" (v. 8).

Jesus compares the incessant, persistent, even rude knocking at a neighbor's door at night to the holy act of faithful prayer. Strangely, he invites us to bother God, to pray, and pray persistently. Don't give up. "Keep buzzing the nurse."[4]

In his letter to the Christians dispersed throughout the Roman Empire because of persecution, the apostle James writes about desire. He warns these believers that their fights and quarrels with each other are owed to their warring desires. "You desire and do not have, so you murder. You covet and cannot obtain, so you fight and quarrel" (James 4:2). Competing desires in that church, as in many churches today, were driving a deep divide between congregants and fueling instinctual jealousy, envy, even hatred. Runaway desire was proving disastrous for their community.

We could imagine James reasonably advising the church to want less. Couldn't they smother the flames of relational conflict if they all assumed a milder, meeker manner that imitated something closer to ambivalence? Wouldn't it simply be easier if they all assumed a want-less, ask-less policy? In exchange for desire, couldn't they have peace?

But this isn't James's advice at all. "You do not have, because you do not ask" (James 4:2). The trouble wasn't that they wanted; the trouble was that they failed to ask God for those desires. Or if they did pray, they often did so with ulterior motives: "You ask and do not receive, because you ask wrongly, to spend it on your passions. You adulterous people! Do you not know that friendship with the world is enmity with God? Therefore whoever wishes to be a friend of the world makes himself an enemy of God" (James 4:3-4). Desire wasn't the problem; idolatry was.

On several different occasions in the Gospels, Jesus asks people what they want: the mother of James and John (Matthew 20:21), James and John themselves (Mark 10:36), blind Bartimaeus (Mark 10:51), and another blind beggar (Luke 18:41). He knew that probing into each of these people's desire was an important means of illuminating their spiritual condition. It was the first step of getting somewhere. Ruth Haley Barton has written in her book *Sacred Rhythms* that our spiritual journey "begins as we learn to pay attention to our desire in God's presence, allowing our desire to become the impetus for deepening our spiritual journey." She insists that we can't rush past the question of desire and distance ourselves from it just "because we are suspicious and afraid of its power."[5]

There are reasons for suspicion: our over-desires (language the Bible uses and which our English translations render as "passions" and "evil desires"), like high-speed trains and supersonic jets, catapult us toward greed and lust. Our under-desires, sluggish as worn-out mules, lope along with a lukewarm, uninspiring kind of ambivalence, of the Laodicean breed. Jesus had stirring words of condemnation for this kind of pallid faith: "Because you are lukewarm, and neither hot nor cold, I will spit you out of my mouth. For you say, I am rich, I have prospered, and I need nothing" (Revelation 3:16-17). We have to be wary of both extremes. Desire can race. Desire can putter. Neither is the proper speed.

§

There is a biblical case for wanting, and wanting well, and I hope I have made it clear in these pages. Although easily corrupted, desire is good, right and necessary. It is a force of movement in our lives, a means of transportation. It can be the very thing that motivates us to change and that carries us to God. Growing into maturity doesn't mean abandoning our desires, but growing in our discernment of them. We are granted the courage to want, but we are also granted the understanding that getting our heart's desire, when idolatrous, can be our greatest tragedy. "Why is getting your heart's deepest desire so often a disaster?" asks Tim Keller in his book *Counterfeit Gods*. "It is because our hearts fashion these desires into idols. . . .

> *Growing into maturity doesn't mean abandoning our desires, but growing in our discernment of them.*

Every human being must live for something. Something must capture our imaginations, our heart's most fundamental allegiance and hope. But the Bible tells us, without the intervention of the Holy Spirit, that object will never be God himself."[6] When God disappoints our idolatrous desires, we can offer profound gratitude for his jealousy. Not getting what we want can be salvation indeed.

The real remediation for sin is the renovation of desire: we must learn to want God and to desire his kingdom coming. In a profound sermon by nineteenth-century Scottish theologian Thomas Chalmers, titled "The Expulsive Power of a New Affection," we learn why desire cannot be conquered and must instead be tamed; why we can't leave off wanting and instead have to learn to want better things.

> If the way to disengage the heart from the positive love of one great and ascendant object, is to fasten it in positive love to another, then it is not by exposing the worthlessness of the former, but by addressing to the mental eye the worth and excellence of the latter, that all old things are to be done away and all things are to become new.[7]

To love the world less is possible only as we begin to love Christ more. And we love Christ more as we consider his love for us.

Great Expectations

It's a story I've heard many times. Only the characters and minor details of the plot change. Someone has had a crisis of faith. They've gone off declaring that they no longer believe in Jesus, the Bible, that this had all been the stuff of their childhood, imbibed and ingested, a spoon-fed faith from the hands of their well-meaning parents. The crisis of faith is like a coming of age, where they outgrow Christian orthodoxy and try on the world for size. Only it isn't just faith that falls in this cataclysmic shift of worldview. The aftershocks of tearing at the philosophic foundations of life bring down other buildings too.

Recently, a friend told me how she'd learned that a close colleague from her Christian corporation had left his wife and three children. "I'm not a Christian anymore. I simply can't pretend that I am," this man had explained to my friend. She listened sympathetically, acknowledging that it would indeed be difficult to repair his marriage if his wife insisted on Christian counseling, terms to which he could no longer agree.

It's a week later that my friend learns he's having more than a crisis of faith. He's having an affair.

We might wonder of this man's story: did the crisis of faith precipitate the moral one? Or had the crisis of faith been necessary for the moral crisis? Faith—and the moral will of God—insists we, as sinful human beings, can't have everything we may want.

When Jesus insists on a firm and unwavering no, we always have a choice. In the words of Father Mapple, the preacher in Melville's *Moby-Dick,* the freedom is ours to "disobey ourselves."

§

"Teacher, what good deed must I do to have eternal life?" asks the rich young man of Jesus.

"If you would enter life, keep the commandments," replies Jesus as he enumerates the divine demands: You shall not murder, you shall not commit adultery, you shall not steal, you shall not bear false witness, honor your father and mother, love your neighbor as yourself. "All these I have kept," insists the rich young man. But sensing his spiritual deficit, he asks, "What do I still lack?"

"If you would be perfect," Jesus continued, "go, sell what you possess and give to the poor, and you will have treasure in heaven; and come, follow me."

This man is given the choice: to disobey his own desires for personal comfort. Sadly, he despises the holy freedom Jesus offers to him and "went away sorrowful, for he had great possessions" (Matthew 19:16-22).

&

I have feared these stories could become mine: the man who abandoned faith and ended his marriage, the rich young ruler who hung himself on the love of money. I know my heart wanders restlessly and pines to fulfill its deepest vanities. My instincts are strong for self-preservation and self-love. I am a woman deeply afraid to want, a woman who has even felt that the fear of wanting has kept her safe.

I would let go and fall far from this rescue of grace.

At sixteen, this is what fear was telling me. Twenty years later, I was still listening.

I have needed, again and again, chapter after chapter, to preach the gospel to myself because I believe this good news is the antidote to fear. It nudges us to believe more deeply that we are, on no merit of our own, *saved.* At the age of sixteen, I gave myself, as fully as I knew how, into the capable, saving hands of Jesus. And what does Scripture tell me about the kind of salvation Jesus effects on behalf of those who, by faith through grace alone, put their trust in him? "He is able to save to the uttermost those who draw near to God through him, since he always lives to make intercession for them" (Hebrews 7:25). I had a merciful and faithful high priest, a God willing to love me when I was yet his enemy, a God committed to loving me despite my future treacheries of desire.

And he had great expectations.

In *Booked,* in the chapter "The Magic of Story: Great Expectations," Karen Swallow Prior describes the grace of God as his "great expectations" of and for his people. Dickens's novel *Great Expectations* tells the story of Pip, an orphan who, having come into an inheritance later in life, despises the poor blacksmith Joe, who had raised Pip as his own son. When Pip falls ill and Joe nurses him back to health, Pip realizes his great error in rejecting the father figure who has loved him so persistently and sacrificially. "'Oh, Joe, you break my heart! Look angry at me, Joe. Strike me, Joe. Tell me of my ingratitude. Don't be so good to me!' For Joe had actually laid his head down on the pillow at my side, and put his arm round my neck, in his joy that I knew him."

Prior says, "Surely, this is a picture of God, who is said to be longsuffering, stretching out his hand for us to grasp the very moment we will."[8]

It has required more than tens of thousands of words, but I am growing to believe this more confidently—that God, and his great expectations, are strong enough to hold, even when I want, and want wrongly. And though we surprise ourselves, we never surprise God, nor do we, because of our betrayals, separate ourselves from the love of God in Christ. "Who shall bring any charge against God's elect? It is God who justifies. Who is to condemn? Christ Jesus is the one who died—more than that, who was raised—who is at the right hand of God, who indeed is interceding for us. Who shall separate us from the love of Christ?" (Romans 8:33-35). The gospel invites me to risk want.

Risk Boldly

My father-in-law once told me, "I think you'll write a book." He was one of many, especially those in the church, who believed long before I did that writing was one of the cups of cold water I had to offer the world in the name of Christ. I am infinitely grateful that God has spoken his "great expectations" through them because I have needed them to believe not only that this work is good but that I am good for wanting this work.

"Writing has to do with darkness, and a desire or perhaps a compulsion to enter it, and, with luck, to illuminate it, and to bring something back out to the light," says Margaret Atwood in her book *Negotiating with the Dead*.[9] After moving to Toronto, I did exactly what Atwood suggests. Understanding little of where I was headed, knowing only that I had the desire to travel, those stories took me somewhere.

They dared me to bravely take up my own acts of honesty. They exposed my fears about desire. They eventually led me deeper into grace. And I trust these pages have reeled you in closer to the ownership of your own stories and desires, although they—and we—will often seem wayward. Grace alone dares us to affirm that God holds fast to hope for us when we may have long ago given ourselves up. Grace alone meets the fears of desire.

The church, in its practice of grace and affirmation of "great expectations," helps and heals in direct measure to its willingness to bear, like Christ, the telling of our stories. The church can walk faithfully alongside us in our journey to admit desire. I hope, at the end of this book, we've found ourselves, no matter our calling, willing to want Christ's church—because the church is where I found and took up the desire to write.

"Cast your bread upon the waters, for you will find it after many days. Give a portion to seven, or even to eight, for you know not what disaster may happen on earth. If the clouds are full of rain, they empty themselves on the earth, and if a tree falls to the south or to the north, in the place where the tree falls, there it will lie. He who observes the wind will not sow, and he who regards the clouds will not reap" (Ecclesiastes 11:1-4). This was the text of our pastor's sermon. He was talking about calling. I wondered about writing.

Calling—or this proverbial act of "casting bread onto water"—is inherently risky, our pastor pointed out.

> The writer is pointing to typical reasons that people use to stop themselves from risking. In an agricultural world, sowing seeds was best done in perfect weather. And so he describes imperfect conditions: rainy weather, fallen trees in the field, wind. And the point of this passage is, there is never a perfect time to risk, to express faith in God. If the conditions were perfect it would not be a risk. Sowing seeds in perfect weather is just sowing—it is not casting your bread on the water.

"The writer of Ecclesiastes says one thing to us," our pastor concluded. "Risk boldly."[10]

Is risk what I feared most in my longing and ambition to write? Was I scared not simply that writing was selfish or self-aggrandizing, but that it committed me to risk? Was I afraid to risk the sound of my own voice, to risk the opinions of others? Would I risk failing— and failing publicly?

"For which of you, *desiring* to build a tower, does not first sit down and count the cost, whether he has enough to complete it?" Jesus once asked his disciples (Luke 14:28). He understood the risk of desire. He knew that on the heels of desire followed commitment. If we were to begin daring to want, what would we begin daring to do? What petitions would our desires inspire? And what plans those petitions?

> May [God] grant you your heart's desire
>   and fulfill all your plans! . . .
> May the Lord fulfill all your petitions! (Psalm 20:4-5)

The psalmist understood that desire would animate faith and faith, action.

What would it be like to step into the world—and call out my hello?

But of course I have done that now. Wanted to write. And written a book. I have risked. I have risked wanting. This book embodies all that is bent and tangled in that process. I concern myself less with fear now, for I think I have found more sure footing—in grace.

Our Father in heaven,
hallowed be your name.
Your kingdom come,
your will be done,
    on earth as it is in heaven.
Give us this day our daily bread,
and forgive us our debts,
    as we also have forgiven our debtors.
And lead us not into temptation,
but deliver us from evil. (Matthew 6:9-13)

Reflection Questions

1. If the gospel rescues us from fear, what spiritual practices drive us more deeply into understanding and appreciating this good news?

2. If you were to begin daring to want, what would you begin daring to do?

3. What petitions would your holiest desires inspire? What plans would those petitions generate?

4. How do you view desire differently now, having read this book?

Acknowledgments

I was thirty-five weeks pregnant when the doctor performed the last of my ultrasounds on a Friday morning in the middle of January. "You're ready to go anytime!" The twins were born the following morning, both fully cooked at five pounds.

Andrew slid first through the birth canal—before the doctor was scrubbed up. "Stop laughing!" he chided. But then the minutes ticked by, and the assembled team of doctors and nurses for Baby B stood silently by, listening worriedly to his heart rate. We held our collective breath when the pace slowed like a tired mule—thump . . . thump . . . thump. We exhaled relief when it galloped again—thump-thump-thump-thump. But an hour of listening, an hour of tense, quiet conversations between my obstetrician and the anesthesiologist (conversations from which I was unapologetically excluded), and finally Colin was born by C-section, the umbilical cord looped around his waist and over his shoulder, his little fingers clutching it with characteristic intensity.

❧

The writing was cooked. And yet, it took a team of strong hands to deliver it.

First, I want to thank Tom Bennardo, pastor of Life Community Church, in Hilliard, Ohio. When, in 2003, I caught the wild idea to write and suggested to him a project I might undertake for the church, he heartily agreed. It was badly written, but Tom never let on. I am grateful.

In 2004, that devotional project provided a writing sample for the wonderful team at *Today in the Word*, whose managing editor, Heather Moffitt, has now been a longtime friend. Without the generous encouragement from the editors and readers of *Today in the Word*, this book simply would not be.

Still, a near-decade of devotional writing, and I lacked confidence and clarity for this calling. The good people at Grace Toronto Church provided the theological understanding—and community— I needed to reconcile the holy desires for art and worship. Thank you, Ian Cusson, for your important work with Grace Centre for the Arts. And thank you, Dan MacDonald and Kyle Hackmann, for the serious theological reflection you bring to our congregation each week. We are blessed.

Wendy, whom I met at Grace Toronto Church, has not only received many of my confessions, she's also read many early (and bad) versions of this book. This trusted friend is also a fantastic writer, and I can't wait for you to read her book.

It is my great joy that Katelyn Beaty agreed to write the foreword to this book, for it was her patient help, when I first began pitching to *Christianity Today*, that provided much-needed encouragement— to try and try again. Also, Chris Smith, author of *Slow Church* and editor of *The Englewood Review of Books*, has been an invaluable friend and source of professional advice. It was he who made my introduction to Dave Zimmerman, IVP's editor extraordinaire. When Dave agreed to review my proposal and, further, helped improve it, I received it as unexpected grace.

To me, each of you has been Christ. And he is the one I long to honor in these pages.

But before the list grows infinitely long, let me thank the people whom I cherish most, my husband and my children. Audrey, Nathan, Camille, Andrew, Colin and even now, James: you have eaten your fair share of store-bought rotisserie chickens in order that I might finish this work. I thank you for your patience and your full-hearted enthusiasm for this project. Ryan: as you are the man I most admire, yours is the confidence I most need. Thank you for your steadfast love these eighteen years. And whatever we agree together to call my writing life, with you, I look forward to calling it good.

Discussion Guide

1. The author describes her mistaken theology of desire. "I [had] wanted to believe that desire [was] bad, that I [was] bad for wanting" (chap. 1). Are these notions about desire common in the church? If so, why?

2. If secular culture attests to the "unqualified goodness of desire" (chap. 2), what different claims is this book making?

3. The author cites the evangelical church's overconfidence in right "thinking" for the process of discipleship (chap. 2). Do you agree or disagree that in its treatment of our "disordered loves" (Augustine), "the church is pouring water on our head to put out a fire in our heart" (James K. A. Smith)? Give examples from your own church experience.

4. The book describes desire as a key ingredient to our spiritual transformation. "The simple question, 'What do I want?' can lead to important change. . . . Ignoring our desires may serve as the convenient way we remain ignorant and resist change" (chap. 2). How might the exploration of desire affect profound spiritual change?

5. In every chapter, the author returns to grace, claiming that by virtue of God's steadfast and forgiving love, he rescues us from our faithless desires. "Yes, I would want wrong things—and God would persist in loving me still" (chap. 3). Is this the abuse of grace to which Paul refers in Romans 6:1, where he asks, "Are we to continue in sin that grace may abound?" If not, what might be the difference?

6. In chapter four, the author describes how the gospel was first proclaimed to her: "God has a wonderful plan for your life." She then describes moving into a fuller understanding of the gospel: "God has a wonderful plan for the world." What difference does this ultimately make for the content and character of holy desire?

7. If selfishness and greed are to be avoided, the author suggests we burrow into greater trust. "Trust is at the center of holy desire: trust that God is good and wills good for his people. . . . Holy trust believes that whatever God chooses to give is enough" (chap. 4). What is the process by which we can grow into greater trust?

8. Learning the language of holy desire is something that happens when we keep company with other Christians. "Let us consider how to stir up one another to love and good works, not neglecting to meet together, as is the habit of some, but encouraging one another, and all the more as you see the Day drawing near," bids the writer of Hebrews (10:24-25). Why are God's people so critical to navigating the terrain of our own heart's desires?

9. The author claims that her stories of loss are critically important to a balanced and biblical discussion of desire. "Maybe [they] are the most credible stories I have to tell" (chap. 10). Why is loss and disappointment necessary for a life of holy desire?

10. The book hangs loosely on the structure of the Lord's Prayer, suggesting that holy desire is formed by practices like Scripture reading, prayer, petition, confession and community. "Though daily spiritual disciples could reduce the desire for God into dry, perfunctory routine, in my own life they inaugurated a beautiful, nearly invisible process of rehabilitation" (chap. 5). How do we reconcile the importance of God's grace *and* our intentional practices, particularly for the renovation of our desires?

11. The author suggests that prayer, at its best, is brave and authentic. We should learn to meet God in our "doubt and desire, praise and perplexity, fear and failure" (chap. 6). Is this view of prayer supported by Scripture? In your experience, is it welcome in our churches?

12. The author maintains her own "pact of transparency" (chap. 8) by telling many of her own stories of desire in the book. This candor is crucial, she says. But if honest self-appraisal is so vital for exploring desire—and as difficult as Dan Ariely suggests (see chapter 8)—what hope do we have of ever honestly discerning the true nature of our desires?

13. There are two great sins of extreme in the case of human desire. Either we want too little from God or we want too much. Catalog what kinds of sins grow out of wanting too little and out of wanting too much. Consider anger, bitterness, idolatry, jealousy, sexual immorality, dishonesty, pride, unforgiveness, gluttony, sloth and lust.

14. Storytelling emerges as a theme in the book, and the author defends that "[our desires] tell a part of the story that God is telling through us, even the beautiful and complicated story of being human and becoming holy" (chap. 10). Must every Christian, whether or not she is a writer, "keep her story"? What is lost if those stories aren't rehearsed, preserved and shared?

15. In the final chapter, the author reads Psalm 20 and suggests two biblical fruits of holy desire: petitions and plans. What does desire look like without holy petitions and plans? What do petitions and plans look like without holy desire?

Notes

Chapter 1: Afraid to Want
[1]Madeleine L'Engle, *Circle of Quiet* (New York: HarperCollins, 1972), p. 21.
[2]Elizabeth Gilbert, *Eat, Pray, Love* (New York: Penguin, 2006), p. 92.
[3]Edith Wharton, *House of Mirth* (New York: Signet Classics, 2000), p. 6.
[4]Josef Pieper, *Leisure: The Basis of Culture* (South Bend, IN: St. Augustine's Press, 1998), p. 36.
[5]Ibid., p. 37.

Chapter 2: Aperture of the Heart
[1]Rachel Cusk, *A Life's Work* (New York: Picador, 2002), p. 8.
[2]Lizzie Widdicombe, "The Plagiarist's Tale," *The New Yorker,* February 13, 2012.
[3]Brennan Manning, *The Ragamuffin Gospel* (Portland, OR: Multnomah, 1990), p. 22.
[4]Christopher Hitchens, "Fetal Distraction," *Vanity Fair,* February 2003.
[5]Tim Keller, *The Reason for God* (New York: Dutton, 2008), p. 159.
[6]Annie Dillard, *Pilgrim at Tinker Creek* (New York: HarperCollins, 1998), p. 30.
[7]Eugene Peterson, *Eat This Book: A Conversation in the Art of Spiritual Reading* (Grand Rapids: Eerdmans, 2006), p. 57.
[8]James K. A. Smith, *Desiring the Kingdom* (Grand Rapids: Baker Academic, 2009), p. 77.

Chapter 3: Precipice of Hope
[1]C. S. Lewis, *The Great Divorce*, in *The Complete C. S. Lewis Signature Classics* (New York: HarperCollins, 2002), p. 506.
[2]James K. A. Smith, *Desiring the Kingdom* (Grand Rapids: Baker Academic, 2009). See chap. 1, "Homo Liturgicus: The Human Person as Lover."
[3]Ibid., pp. 52, 54.

[4]Ibid., p. 91.

[5]N. T. Wright, *The Lord and His Prayer* (Grand Rapids: Eerdmans, 1997), p. 2.

[6]Eric Metaxas, *Bonhoeffer* (Nashville: Thomas Nelson, 2010), chap. 5 (Kindle ed.).

[7]Mary Karr, *Lit* (New York: HarperCollins, 2009), p. 234.

[8]Ibid., p. 241.

[9]Ibid., p. 275.

[10]Philip Yancey, "Does Prayer Change God?" *Books and Culture*, September/ October 2005.

Chapter 4: Project Kingdom

[1]Abraham Kuyper, inaugural lecture, Free University of Amsterdam (1880).

[2]N. T. Wright, *What Saint Paul Really Said* (Grand Rapids: Eerdmans, 1997), p. 154.

[3]Ibid., p. 157.

[4]Eric Metaxas, *Bonhoeffer* (Nashville: Thomas Nelson, 2010), p. 81.

[5]Ibid.

[6]Madeleine L'Engle, *Circle of Quiet* (New York: HarperCollins, 1979), p. 218.

[7]John H. Sailhamer, *The Pentateuch as Narrative* (Grand Rapids: Zondervan, 1992), p. 134.

[8]Ibid., p. 135.

[9]Rachel Marie Stone, *Eat with Joy* (Downers Grove, IL: InterVarsity Press, 2013), chap. 1 (Kindle ed.).

[10]Ibid., p. 136.

[11]Jen Pollock Michel, "How a Korean Prodigal Son Landed on Toronto's Stage," *Christianity Today*, December 12, 2012.

Chapter 5: Visions of Sugarplums

[1]This phrase "Now one foot, now the other" is the title of a children's book by Tomie dePaola. The grandfather teaches little Bobby to walk, telling him, "Now one foot, now the other." When the grandfather suffers a stroke several years later, it's Bobby teaching the grandfather to walk, coaxing him, "Now one foot, now the other."

[2]Tim Keller, *Counterfeit Gods* (New York: Riverhead, 2009), p. 37.

[3]Ibid., p. 38.

[4]Joan Didion, *The Year of Magical Thinking* (New York: Alfred A. Knopf, 2006), p. 3.

[5]Ann Voskamp, *One Thousand Gifts* (Grand Rapids: Zondervan, 2010), p. 68.

[6]Ibid., p. 10.

[7]Stanley Hauerwas, *Hannah's Child* (Grand Rapids: Eerdmans, 2010), p. 137.

[8]C. S. Lewis, *A Grief Observed*, in *The Complete C.S. Lewis Signature Classics* (New York: HarperCollins, 2002), p. 653.

[9]Caitlin Flanagan, "The Autumn of Joan Didion," *The Atlantic*, December 20, 2011.

[10]Keller, *Counterfeit Gods*, p. 20.

[11]T. M. Luhrmann, *When God Talks Back* (New York: Vintage, 2012), p. 130.

Chapter 6: The Business of Holy

[1]Eugene Peterson, *The Jesus Way* (Grand Rapids: Eerdmans, 2007), p. 132.

[2]Mary Karr, "Revelations in the Key of K," in *Sinners Welcome* (New York: HarperCollins, 2006), p. 2.

[3]N. T. Wright, *What Saint Paul Really Said* (Grand Rapids: Eerdmans, 1997), p. 111.

[4]C. S. Lewis, *Mere Christianity*, in *The Complete C. S. Lewis Signature Classics* (New York: HarperCollins, 2002), p. 152.

[5]Eugene Peterson, *Practice Resurrection* (Grand Rapids: Eerdmans, 2010), p. 96.

[6]Philip Yancey, "Does Prayer Change God?" *Books and Culture*, September/October 2005.

[7]Mary Karr, *Lit* (New York: HarperCollins, 2009), p. 247.

Chapter 7: Bread and Butter

[1]G. K. Chesterton, *The Everlasting Man* (San Francisco: Ignatius, 1993), p. 133.

[2]William Cavanaugh, *Being Consumed* (Grand Rapids: Eerdmans, 2008), p. 11.

[3]Saint Augustine, *Confessions* (New York: Oxford University Press, 1998), p. 30.

[4]Kathleen Norris, "The Quotidian Mysteries" (New York: Paulist, 1998), Kindle ed.

[5]N. T. Wright, *The Lord and His Prayer* (Grand Rapids: Eerdmans, 1997), p. 41.

[6]Ibid., p. 42.

[7]Frederick Buechner, *Whistling in the Dark* (New York: HarperCollins, 1993), p. 84.

[8]Bruce Milne, *The Message of John* (Downers Grove, IL: InterVarsity Press, 1993), p. 63.
[9]Wright, *The Lord and His Prayer*, pp. 6-7, 36.

Chapter 8: If the Shoe Fits
[1]Ruth Haley Barton, *Sacred Rhythms* (Downers Grove, IL: InterVarsity Press, 2006), introduction (Kindle ed.).
[2]Andy Crouch, Afterword, in *unChristian* (Grand Rapids: Baker, 2007), p. 230.
[3]Tim Keller, *The Freedom of Self-Forgetfulness* (Chorley, UK: 10Publishing, 2012), chap. 3 (Kindle ed.).
[4]Dan Ariely, *The (Honest) Truth About Dishonesty* (New York: Harper, 2012), chap. 1 (Kindle ed.).
[5]Ibid., chap. 10.
[6]St. Augustine, *Confessions* (New York: Oxford University Press, 1998), p. 145.
[7]Megan Hill, "The Very Worst Trend Ever," *Christianity Today*, July 8, 2013.
[8]Tim Keller, *The Reason for God* (New York: Dutton, 2008), p. 160.
[9]Nathaniel Hawthorne, *The Scarlet Letter* (New York: Vintage, 1990), p. 61.
[10]C. S. Lewis, *The Weight of Glory* (New York: HarperCollins, 2001), p. 26.
[11]Eugene Peterson, *Eat This Book* (Grand Rapids: Eerdmans, 2006), p. 32.
[12]John Piper, *Desiring God* (Colorado Springs: Multnomah, 2011), introduction (Kindle ed.).

Chapter 9: Be My Neighbor
[1]Tim Keller, *The Meaning of Marriage* (New York: Dutton, 2011), p. 36.
[2]Wendell Berry, "Sex, Economy, Freedom and Community," in *Sex, Economy, Freedom and Community* (New York: Pantheon, 1992), p. 149.
[3]Ibid., p. 139.
[4]Julia Scatliff O'Grady, *Good Busy* (Durham, NC: RCMWS, 2012), chap. 6 (Kindle ed.).
[5]David Brooks, "Freedom Loses One," *The New York Times*, April 1, 2013.
[6]Stephen Marche, "Is Facebook Making Us Lonely?" *The Atlantic*, April 2, 2012.
[7]Ibid.
[8]David Kinnaman and Gabe Lyons, *unChristian* (Grand Rapids: Baker, 2007), p. 220.

[9]Thomas C. Oden, *Life in the Spirit,* vol. 3, Systematic Theology (New York: HarperCollins, 1992), p. 282.

[10]James K. A. Smith, *Desiring the Kingdom* (Grand Rapids: Baker Academic, 2009), p. 62.

[11]Ibid., p. 135.

[12]Dietrich Bonhoeffer, *Life Together* (New York: HarperCollins, 1954), p. 20.

[13]Eric Metaxas, *Bonhoeffer* (Nashville: Thomas Nelson, 2010), chap. 21 (Kindle ed.).

[14]Bonhoeffer, *Life Together,* p. 23.

[15]Ibid., p. 22.

[16]Ibid., p. 20.

Chapter 10: Ruby Slippers

[1]Paul Miller, *A Praying Life* (Colorado Springs: NavPress, 2009), p. 24.

[2]Ibid., p. 49.

[3]Kathleen Norris, "The Quotidian Mysteries" (New York: Paulist, 1998), (Kindle ed.).

[4]John Piper, *Desiring God* (Colorado Springs: Multnomah, 2011), chap. 6.

[5]Ruth Haley Barton, *Sacred Rhythms* (Downers Grove, IL: InterVarsity Press, 2006), chap. 1 (Kindle ed.).

[6]Tim Keller, *Counterfeit Gods* (New York: Riverhead, 2009), p. 3.

[7]Thomas Chalmers, "The Expulsive Power of a New Affection," (Kindle ed.).

[8]Karen Swallow Prior, *Booked* (Ossining, NY: T. S. Poetry Press, 2012), chap. 4 (Kindle ed.).

[9]Margaret Atwood, *Negotiating with the Dead* (New York: Anchor, 2002), p. xxiv.

[10]Dan MacDonald, Grace Toronto Church. Used by permission.